Worcestershire, the Haunted County

Worcestershire, the Haunted County

Anne Bradford

BREWIN BOOKS

First published in Great Britain
by Hunt End Books 2007

This edition published by
Brewin Books Ltd, 56 Alcester Road,
Studley, Warwickshire B80 7LG in 2017
www.brewinbooks.com

ISBN: 978-1-85858-566-6

A Cataloguing in Publication Record
for this title is available from the British Library

Printed in Great Britain by
4edge Ltd.

THE AUTHOR AND THE ILLUSTRATOR

Anne Bradford

This is Anne's eighth collection of ghost stories. She has also co-authored one book with David Taylor and three books with the late Barrie Roberts. Her interest began when she accidentally found a Victorian collection of ghostly tales in the local library. She was persuaded by the librarians to publish her first book, and was helped by her husband, a graphic designer. In addition, she has compiled and published three oral history books. She gives talks on a range of subjects which enable her to collect information for her next book.

Anne is a retired teacher of English and commercial subjects. She has three adult children and one grandson.

Zora Payne BA (Hons), Artist/Illustrator

Zora is a professional artist and illustrator. As well as illustrating books, magazines and educational material, she teaches art, paints murals, and runs drawing and craft workshops for adults and children. She also undertakes private commissions. She has a key interest in the story-telling potential of illustration and is well-known for her detailed 'this is your life' portraits. Her speciality is fantasy pictures.

Front cover: Zora's drawing of the terrified lady seen running into the road near Spetchley. See page 155.

CONTENTS

Worcester

The Battle of Worcester   1-6
Bloodstains - The Commandery   7
The Barley Mow, Sidbury   8
The Enchanted Wood   9
The Helpful Entity - Worcester Cathedral   12
Hullo and Goodbye - Barbourne   15
Nightmares at Tudor House - Friar Street   16
Communications from Another World   17
Visitors in the Severn Traveller   18
The Haunted Bus   20
The Haunted Holiday   20
A Slip in Time   21

Alcester   23
Dead Ringer   23
Leave Me Alone!   24
A Holy Ghost   25

Bromsgrove   26
Bromsgrove and Charles Stuart   26
Cavaliers in the Ladies' Loo   27
The Ghosts of Grafton Manor   28
Hell for Leather   29
Precognition - or What?   30
A Clip Round the 'Earole   31

Droitwich   33
Beauty and the Bakers   34
The Black Pudding Apparition   35
A House-proud Entity   36
Jinxed Money Boxes   37
The Haunted Family   38

Evesham   43
Evesham in the Civil War   43
Royalty at the Royal Oak   44

A Wee Experience   46
Bengeworth
The Story of the Ring   47
The Evesham Hotel   48
Blood on His Hands   50

Kidderminster   53
Kidderminster, Rev Baxter and the Civil War   53
Ghosts at the Kidderminster Shuttle   55
Walking Through the Wall   57
Oliver Twist at Castle Road   58
The Crazy Draught   58
The Family Ghost   59
Glowing Hands   60

Malvern   61
Madresfield Court   61
Malvern's Martyr Saint   62
The Intruder   63
The Shadow of Raggedstone Hill   63
The Malvern Beast   65
Screams from a Baby   66
It Wasn't Possums   67
The Flight   68
The Suckley Hills   69
Happily Haunted   69
The Phantom Burglar   71

Pershore   73
Pershore and the Civil War   73
The High Street Coach and Horses   73
The Highwayman and the Angel   74
A Final Note   76

Redditch   77
Strange Goings-On at Forge Mill   77
A Pair of Eyes   80
A Sporting Apparition   81
Flowers for a Baby   85
Skipping Time - Enfield   89

The Prophecy - Batchley   90
Romans in Redditch   93
The White Lady of the Home - Headless Cross   94
The Tragic Friend   95
Boney's Island - Crabbs Cross and Hunt End   95
The Strange Bedfellow   96
Possessed Ballerinas - Oakenshaw   97
Behind the Fireplace - Woodrow   99
The Psychic Student - Winyates Green   100
The Fluid that Flew - Alexandra Hospital   101
A Haunted Honeymoon   101

Stourport-on-Severn   103
A Mysterious Force   103
The Night Visitor   104
Let Your Next Move Be Ours   105
Hartlebury and the Civil War   106

Upton-on-Severn   107
Upton-on-Severn in the Civil War   107
The Haunts of Captain Bounds   108
The Labourer at School - Ripple (and the battle)   110

Worcestershire Villages   113
In the Civil War   113
Alvechurch - *A Child Out of Time*   114
St Laurence's - The Visitor   116
Astwood Bank - *The Ghost on Stilts*   116
In Your Dreams   118
Bishampton - *Two Black Eyes*   120
Bartley Green Reservoir - *The Night Shade*   122
Beoley - *Leave Me Alone*   123
Bretforton   125
Tales from Reverend Shawcross   125
Stately Haunts   126
Broadheath (Upper) - *The Black Orb*   131
Dunhampton - *The Leaking Well*   131
Flyford Flavel - *The Boot, the Dairy and the Poltergeist* 134
Hagley - *Mourning Glory*   136
Hanbury - *Gallows Green*   137

Inkberrow - *The Executioner* 139
Kings Norton - *Manic Raps and Doppelganger Cats* 140
Ledbury - *The Lone Rider* 144
Martin Hussingtree - *Smashes and Crashes* 145
Powick - *'They that shall not grow old'* 147
Rowney Green - *Pestilence Lane* 148
Salford Priors and Abbots Salford 149
Salford Hall and the Queen's Head (Iron Cross)
Sedgeberrow - *The Living Ghost* 151
Spetchley - White Ladies and Peopleton
The Bloody Paintings 153
White Ladies and Dark Deeds 154
The White Lady of White Ladies 155
Studley - *Prayers and Miracles* 157
Stoke Prior - *What the Milkman Saw* 158
Tardebigge - *'Nature's Soft Nurse'* 159
Warndon - *The Old Man and the Child* 160
Wychbold - *The Eerie Airship* 162

Secret Venues
The Mental Hospital 164
The Care Home 167

Epilogue - The Last of King Charles 173

Bibliography and other useful information 174

* An asterisk after a name denotes not real name.

Photographs of Civil War re-enactments by Helen Lee of 'Discover History'.

INTRODUCTION

Oliver Cromwell, Parliamentarian, Leader of the New Model Army.

Charles Stuart, son of Charles I, later Charles II, who brought an army from Scotland in 1651.

Worcester has the dubious privilege of having a battle named after it. This was no skirmish, but one of the greatest battles of English history, when an estimated 3,000 lost their lives. Most towns and villages in Worcestershire were involved in one way or another both in the Battle of Worcester (1651) and in the preceding Civil War of 1642-1646.

To quote the historian Willis Bund,

Worcestershire is one of the smaller English Counties. Its greatest length is but 43 miles, its width 34.... Yet in this confined space more fighting went on during the great Civil War than in most other Counties. ...In every year of the war there was more or less fighting within it.

Paranormal researchers have suggested that violent events can somehow be impregnated into the environment and appropriately sensitive individuals can see or hear a replay of these events.

David Taylor, Chairman and Investigations Co-ordinator of Parasearch, writes:

It is a commonly held belief among paranormal investigators that apparitions are some sort of 'tape recording', somehow recorded onto the very fabric of a building. The theory became popular through the support of Sir Oliver Lodge, Professor of Physics and Mathematics at Liverpool University, later the first Principal of Birmingham University and an eminent Victorian Paranormal Investigator. Lodge suggested that grief and suffering are recorded in some way at the place where they are experienced, and that this process can, later on, produce an apparition. There has been much speculation as to how this effect, called the 'Stone Tape' theory, (after a 1970s television drama) works, with no-one being able to come up with a completely satisfactory explanation.

However, it does offer an explanation as to why there are so many apparitions that could be associated with the Civil War. Other relevant theories include those of timeslips and electro-magnetic 'hotspots'.

This book records the many ghosts and hauntings in a county that suffered more than most the violence and suffering of the Civil War.

WORCESTER

orcester is a city haunted by the ghost of a great battle. The story of the Battle of Worcester is a tragic tale of misplaced ambition creating immeasurable suffering. This is a tale of heroes and villains, of those who showed unbelievable courage and those who were cowards. It carries stories of treachery, foolishness and greed. The butchery by the victors, the 'men of God', is beyond our imagination and reveals the depths to which mankind can sink.

The Battle of Worcester took place in 1651 and was one of the most important conflicts in English history for many reasons. It was the last great battle to be fought on English soil. It brought to an end the conflict between the Parliamentarians and the Royalists. It destroyed the Royalist army and increased the power of the Parliamentarian army under Oliver Cromwell so that they were able to take over the government. Many of the Royalist soldiers had marched down from Scotland so that eleven thousand Scots never returned home, either killed, imprisoned or transported. Farms lay untended, families starved. It bred in the Scots a hatred of the English which persists in some areas to this day.

The troubles began almost as soon as Charles I came to the throne in 1625. He quarrelled with his Parliament, threw them out and ruled without one for eleven years. Eventually, Parliament managed to get control of the army so that Charles I had either to surrender or fight. He chose the latter. The Civil War between the Royalists and the Parliamentarians lasted from 1641 to 1646 and the main battles were at Edgehill, Newbury, Marston Moor and Naseby. Thousands lost their lives and there is hardly a village in Worcestershire which escaped looting and pillaging by starved and ill-disciplined troops. Charles I was captured, tried, and beheaded in January 1649.

Two years later, the twenty-one year old son of Charles I, Charles Stuart, returned from exile to Scotland. He was crowned King of Scotland at Scone on 1st January 1651. He then raised an army and invaded England. Opposing him was the Parliamentarian Oliver Cromwell, with his reformed New Model army.

After a few skirmishes in the north, Charles Stuart marched southwards for Worcester. He knew that Worcester was fiercely Royalist and hoped to find support there. The Welsh were also sympathetic to the King's cause, providing recruits, supplies and ammunition, and it was easy to get supplies from Wales to Worcester.

We have called the two opposing armies the 'Parliamentarians' and the 'Royalists' to distinguish the two sides. By 'Royalists' we refer to those who supported Charles I then Charles Stuart, the future Charles II, with his Scottish army. However, many of those who supported Charles I refused to join Charles Stuart because of the way in which Scottish soldiers had pillaged in Worcestershire during the earlier civil war. Worcestershire folk had been disgusted by their behaviour. No way would they join their ranks.

Charles reached the northern edge of Worcester on Friday, August 22nd 1651. The city had been occupied by 500 Parliamentarian horsemen but when they heard the whole Royalist army was advancing upon them, they beat a hasty retreat to Gloucester. It is said that the locals were taking pot shots at them through their windows. Charles was met by the Mayor who rode before him to the Guild Hall (which has since been moved and rebuilt) carrying the city sword. Within the Hall, he dropped to his knees and gave the king the keys of the city and the important city mace. The army were footsore and weary, they had marched 300 miles in three weeks. They were given badly-needed new shoes and stockings. There was a celebratory service in the Cathedral but unfortunately the preacher put his foot in it by holding forth in glowing terms about 'Royal Supremacy' when the Scots believed in a 'Covenanted King'.

The following Sunday, orders went out to the constables of the different parishes around to send in men to begin work on the fortifications of Worcester. Salwarpe, for example, was told to send 30 men with spades, shovels and pickaxes by five o'clock on the Monday. A letter written at that time says that the workers 'in a few days fortified it (Worcester) beyond imagination'.

Earthworks were thrown up against the walls. On the northern side of the town (the Foregate), the gate was blocked up. St Martin's gate, to the north-east, was the only exit on that side of the town. To the south, earthworks were

A view of Worces-ter today from the top of Fort Royal.

2

thrown up across the London Road from where Cromwell was expected to attack. Sidbury Gate was situated a little nearer to the town centre than the Commandery, near the canal bridge. It was protected by the main defences, a large star-shaped fort, Fort Royal. It was so huge that the earthworks still exist near the Commandery. This was connected by an earthern rampart to the city walls.

The front line was eight miles long and ran from Powick to Pitchcroft, where the race course is now. Charles divided his army into two. The largest half was kept in the city to man the walls and defend the new fortifications. The other half was sent across the Severn and placed in the large expanse between the Teme and the Severn. Bridges were blown up at Bewdley, Upton, Powick and Bransford.

Charles issued an order on Tuesday, 26th, that all men between 16 and 60 were to fight for him and to join him at Pitchcroft 'to aid in the defence of the throne and the liberties of the country'. Only about 2,000 obeyed his summons. The following day he issued a Royal Manifesto urging people to come forward. There was little, if any, result. He issued a further proclamation and promised to give all the pay arrears of any soldiers who joined him from Cromwell's army. Again, there was no result.

The enterprise was doomed from the start. Charles had only about 16,000 troops whereas Cromwell's army numbered about 28,000. Not only was Charles short of recruits, he had very little money to pay for provisions and ammunition. To make matters worse, his generals could not agree among themselves and were often quarrelling. The reinforcements he expected from Wigan and the north had been intercepted by Cromwell and routed.

Before the event Charles stayed with the Vicar of Inkberrow and left his maps behind (see section on Inkberrow in the chapter on Worcestershire villages). Charles' headquarters may have been King Charles' House in New Street which still exists as a restaurant. A quotation in their brochure reads:

'...During his residence in Worcester, it is said, the King made his headquarters in the Cornmarket, near the north end of New Street, at a large house, parts of which are still standing. Here, in the bedroom fronting the Cornmarket, he held council with his officers, and here, when the battle was over, he was closely pursued by Colonel Cobbit, but effected his escape at the back door (now the front door of the restaurant) just as his pursuers entered the front ...'.

The Restaurant boasts a dungeon on the ground floor where there have been many sightings of ghosts!

As for Cromwell, a few days before the battle he is said to have gone to the

3

house of Mr Justice Berkeley at Spetchley, three miles from Worcester, where he established himself during the subsequent operations. Other accounts say that Mr Berkeley burnt the house down 'sooner than it should be defiled by sheltering a regicide'. However local folklore says that Cromwell spent the night in Nunnery Wood where he sold his soul to the devil for victory and seven years good fortune. It's certainly a strange coincidence that the battle took place on 3rd September 1651 and he died on 3rd September 1658.

Cromwell's priority was to block the gateway to Wales, but his main plan of attack was to force all Charles' army into Worcester, where they would be trapped. If he could get across to the west side of the Severn, where the Royalists were camped, it would help to achieve both of these requirements. Cromwell began to build two makeshift bridges by lashing boats together, one across the Severn and the other across the Teme where the two rivers joined.

To distract the attention of the Scots from the boat-building, Cromwell put one cannon on Red Hill and another in or near Perry Wood to fire on the Royalists. The guns were a considerable nuisance so the Royalists decided to try to capture them. On the night of 31st August two groups of soldiers crept out into the darkness to Perry Wood and Red Hill. It's unbelievable that, for this night attack, they decided to wear white shirts over their breast and back pieces to identify themselves. Unfortunately, there was in the city an unprincipled tailor by the name of Guise who let himself down from the city walls on a rope and informed the Parliamentarians of the plot. They lay in wait for the Royalists who were easy to spot because of their white shirts. The Royalists were taken by surprise and next day eleven bodies were found on the Kempsey Road. Guise was at once arrested and hung. However, his widow became very wealthy. In the years following the battle she received from Parliament a total of about £1,700, to ease her widowhood.

The two makeshift bridges were finished on 2nd September and Cromwell gave orders that the army should attack the next day. On mid-morning of 3rd September, the Parliamentarians leaped into action with their battle cry 'Lord of Hosts!'. The fighting began at Powick Bridge and in Wick fields (near Lower Wick) followed by heavy fighting between Perry Wood, Diglis and the town. Although Charles was outnumbered, battles in history have been won against greater odds and several times the fighting swung in his favour. A great disadvantage for Charles was that he was unable to provide reinforcements. However, at Pitchcroft was a Scottish General, Leslie, with the whole of the Scot Cavalry. Several times he might have saved the day for Charles but he refused to move.

When Charles and his staff heard the guns in action they rushed to the top of the Cathedral tower to watch the fighting. As soon as Charles understood

Cromwell's tactics, he rode off to Powick to tell his soldiers that they must stand firm. Then he visited his contingent south of St John's before he returned to the city. The Royalists fought with incredible bravery but finally they had no choice but to retreat into Worcester city.

As Leslie would not move, it was decided to attack the Parliamentarian strongholds at Red Hill and Perry Wood. Charles gathered all available troops, marched out of Sidbury gate and onto Red Hill, while the Duke of Hamilton led a similar assault on Perry Wood. They succeeded in capturing the guns, and driving back the Parliamentarians, but when Cromwell heard what was taking place, he rushed to support his men, stopping their retreat and ordering them to stand firm. Hamilton's ammunition gave out. He fell, wounded in the leg. Fort Royal was stormed. The troops rushed down the hill to Sidbury gate but the gate was so narrow that only a few could pass at a time. The Royalists could not get outside except through the pikes of the Parliamentarians and they could not get inside. There was total chaos, the Royalists were stuck and it was an easy matter for the Parliamentarians to cut them down. They showed no mercy. A great slaughter took place on this spot.

Charles was at the entrance to the Commandery, before Sidbury gate. It is said that one of Cromwell's troopers recognised him and rode his horse at him. Nearby, a team of oxen attached to a munitions wagon had come to a halt as the driver had been killed. With great presence of mind a man by the name of William Bagnall seized the bridle of the team and pulled them, across the road. This enabled Charles to slip through the narrow space created by the entrance to the Commandery, the city walls and the oxen. It

The remnants of the house where King Charles' made his headquarters. It has now been reno-vated and is a restaurant known as 'King Charles House'.

5

seems unlikely that slow-moving oxen could halt a fast-charging horse but that's the story and Bagnall was well-rewarded for it in later years.

Charles made for his quarters in the Corn Market, probably King Charles' House. The Foregate (north gate) had been blocked up, Sidbury (the south gate) was in the hands of the Parliamentarians, as was the Bridge Gate (the West gate). Friar's gate (to the east) led straight into the Parliamentary lines. The only possible exit was St Martin's gate and fortunately it adjoined his quarters. As the troopers of the Parliamentarians entered the front door, he just managed to slip out the back, mounted a horse held for him by Lord Wilmot and galloped out through St Martin's gate, along a lane to Barbourne Bridge and make his escape.

The Lord of Hosts were victorious. They rampaged through the town, out of control, killing and looting. A letter written on 6th September states:

Things at Worcester are in great confusion. Lords, knights and gentlemen were there plucked out of holes by the soldiers. The common prisoners they were driving into the Cathedral, and what with the dead bodies of the men and dead horses of the enemy filling the streets there was such nastiness that a man could hardly abide in the town. Yet the Lord General had his head-quarters in Worcester, the walls whereof he hath ordered to be pulled down to the ground, and the dykes filled up.

Discover History is a group of Freelance Historical Interpreters who organise historical talks and events. A member of the Society, Paul, remarks:

As the evening fell on the 3rd September 1651, the King was beginning his legendary escape and the Royalists were in full flight across the county. The victorious New Model Army (Parliament) was looking for Royalists. Houses were ransacked and people with no connection with the battle were seized and in some cases killed or beaten. This included women! The City was in its darkest hour, dead littered the streets, gullies ran with blood and wounded cried with pain. Sir Andrew Melvill was a Scotsman like most of the Royalists. He lay unconscious from having his horse shot from under him. As he came around Parliament soldiers were beginning to 'plunder the dead.' An argument broke out between some of the men over who would have what items of his clothes. In the end one soldier fired at him to spoil the doublet to spite the others! He survived, but the wounded Melvill suffered a similar fate when laid up in a house. The very bed he rested on was stolen too! Poor man!!!

The Scottish army comprised approximately 16,000 men. Of these, 3,000 were lying dead, 10,000 were prisoners and 2,000 were fugitives. Many of the dead were buried in the churchyard.

The Commandery

The number of Royalist prisoners were so large the Parliamentarians did not know what to do with them. The prisoners were temporarily kept in the cathedral, where much damage was done. When they left, the Cathedral was disinfected with 'pitch and rosen'. The prisoners were taken to London but the guards were so few that many escaped.

A thousand were sent to Bristol to be transported. The price for a prisoner was so low that the slave market came to a standstill!

The Governor of Worcester was held in Warwick Castle. He was Colonel Henry Washington, an ancestor of George Washington, first President of the United States. The family arms, three stars and five horizontal stripes, formed the basis for the stars and stripes.

It was the end of Worcester as one of England's greatest cities. The town walls were demolished. Churches and houses were in ruins. All the Cathedral buildings had lost the lead and the timber from the roofs. Heavy fines were imposed on every property-owner in the city and the town had been left impoverished. It was not until the 1720s that buildings began to be rebuilt.

It took Worcester 100 years to recover from the war and even then, it never managed to recapture its former glory.

Bloodstains – The Commandery

Founded as a hospital by St Wulstan in 1085, historians say that the nurses were called 'Commanders', hence its name. At the end of the battle, the Commandery was the only building left standing in a sea of rubble and is therefore the best remaining relic of the battle. It was outside the city walls but inside the fortifications. The Duke of Hamilton and some of the Scotch Lords were probably staying here and during the battle it appears to have been used as a field hospital.

The Duke of Hamilton was rallying his troops in Perry Wood when he was shot in the leg. He was carried into the Commandery where the King's surgeon stated that the leg should be amputated. When Cromwell heard that the Duke had been injured, he sent his own surgeon to see to him. While the two surgeons were arguing as to whether or not the leg should

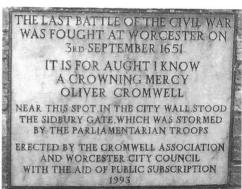

THE LAST BATTLE OF THE CIVIL WAR
WAS FOUGHT AT WORCESTER ON
3RD SEPTEMBER 1651

IT IS FOR AUGHT I KNOW
A CROWNING MERCY
OLIVER CROMWELL

NEAR THIS SPOT, IN THE CITY WALL, STOOD
THE SIDBURY GATE, WHICH WAS STORMED
BY THE PARLIAMENTARIAN TROOPS

ERECTED BY THE CROMWELL ASSOCIATION
AND WORCESTER CITY COUNCIL
WITH THE AID OF PUBLIC SUBSCRIPTION
1993

Left: The Barley Mow, in Sidbury, built on the site of some of the worst fighting in the Battle of Worcester.
Above: The plaque on the wall of the bridge next to the Commandery.

be amputated, the Duke died. According to Willis Bund, 'His blood was in recent years shewn on a board in a room in the ground floor'. Permission was asked to return the body to his home, Hamilton Palace, but refused. Instead he was buried inside Worcester Cathedral wrapped in lead. In 1862, when renovations were going on in the Cathedral, a workman accidentally put a pickaxe through his head.

The Barley Mow, Sidbury

A few yards from the Commandery stands the Barley Mow. It has a Victorian frontage but the back is much older. Again, the site was just outside the city gate but within the fortifications for the town. Some of the fiercest fighting of the Battle of Worcester took place here and when the battle was over, bodies were piled high against the gates. It comes as no surprise to learn that the Barley Mow has a long history of strange happenings. The licensees from 1971 to 1992 heard footsteps at night, they had problems with articles disappearing, locked doors opening and one night a guest saw a dark ghost with long hair in the cellar, thought to be a Royalist.

In 2006, Andrea was the licensee:

The very first time I stayed at the pub I was up in the living room

8

at around 5pm, putting some stuff on the fireplace, when out of the corner of my eye, to the right by the door, I caught sight of a very large and tall black shadow. As I turned to look it disappeared out of the door. Later that night we had a new bed delivered, and as we were busy we left the plastic wrapping on the floor. I was trying to get to sleep but, being in a new place that was supposed to be haunted, was finding it difficult. Now, I'm no chicken usually but I did feel uneasy. I was drifting off when I heard footsteps. The carpet was brand new so when you walked on it, it kind of crunched. I heard somebody walk into the bedroom, walk up to me, look over me, then walk around the bed – I could hear the crunching as they walked over the plastic wrapping - to Graham's side of the bed. He or she stopped to look over him, then walked back over the plastic and out of the room! My heart was racing and I hid under the bedclothes.

These where the two main incidents. The other events were quite minor, like walking downstairs and smelling perfume or sometimes Vicks Vapour rub. I always had a sense of being watched in the living room, and one day when I wasn't well I went to sleep in the living room but kept being woken by the feeling that somebody was looking over me. I always felt uneasy in the cellar, it was very oppressive down there, it was straight down, get what you want and back out asap.

The boiler stopped working for over a week, it was freezing cold in here, and two different engineers from different companies both said it was beyond repair. Then it just fired up all by itself and started to work again. Sometimes I would go to bed and the bar was spotless but when I got up there would be a dirty pint glass at one end of the bar. There were six lights all over the bar on a link, and one morning, I was talking to a customer about these ghosts when one of the light bulbs exploded over his head for no reason.

One lady had a frightening experience in the loos. The lock broke in her hand so that she couldn't open the door and at the same time, the light bulb went. She was stuck in the loo in the dark for fifteen minutes.

Leanne and her partner help out in the bar. She says:

When the licensee found out that she was going to be away overnight, my partner and I offered to stay on the premises. So last Monday, 27th April, after locking up and making sure the premises were secure, we moved into the first floor bedroom.

The Barley Mow is really creepy. Several people have heard or seen something spooky here. I myself have heard footsteps. I'm scared just going round in the day, so I felt quite nervous about staying overnight. I'm a light sleeper, and I kept waking up and hearing the footsteps. You could hear thud, thud, thud, it definitely sounded like somebody walking round but at other times the footsteps would be quicker and lighter. They were quite irregular, sometimes they would go on for about five minutes, sometimes only for two minutes, with a gap inbetween. They seemed to be coming from the hallway and upstairs, mostly the hallway. I dived under the quilt.

Then, in the early hours of the morning, probably at about three o'clock, I heard children giggling. There was definitely more than one child there, perhaps a couple. They weren't teenagers and they weren't toddlers – somewhere between the ages of four and eleven. I was half asleep but I could tell the noise was coming from upstairs, on the second floor. I sat up in bed and thought, 'Oh my God' and kept thumping my partner to wake him up. The giggling only went on for about five or ten seconds before it stopped, so by the time he was awake everything was quiet.

The strange thing is that, at about four o'clock, my partner heard the giggling but I couldn't hear it. I was so tired I dropped off to sleep.

When I got home I told my mum and she said, 'Oh, it's just you', But my gran was very interested and told me about all the spooky things that had happened to her.

The Enchanted Wood

John and Carol live in a house on the edge of Perry Wood

Our house is on the edge of Perry Wood, where a lot of the fighting of the Civil War took place. Although the house is fairly new, the local historian tells us it was built on the site of an old farm. Since we have moved into this house all kinds of strange things have happened. The light bulbs pop all the time, I can't tell you how many we have replaced recently. I often find it difficult to sleep and I was lying awake one night, I turned over and on the bedroom wall was a big image of a canon of the type used in the civil war. The cannon was a couple of feet across and had gone rusty. It was pale grey with a longish base and I could see clearly the big screws to hold the cannon on. I lay there, watching it for a few minutes. Then I said to myself, 'Don't be silly, it's your imagination' and when I turned back the cannon had gone.

My father died seven years previously and I was very close to him.

Once I got the impression that he was saying, 'Don't go into that part of the wood, it's very dangerous', so I didn't go. A few days later a young lady was attacked there. Whether that was anything to do with it I don't know.

A memorable incident happened recently. We breed dogs, we take the dogs for walks in the wood. We have one litter each year and I am very particular who they go to. I like to know that each animal is going to a good home. I had a male puppy and the people who said they wanted it let me down at the last minute, but they said they had a friend who would like it. I told them to send him along. To my amazement the phone went only a few minutes later and he was on the motorway coming to our house. My son was upstairs and my husband was out.

He came in and I didn't like him at all. He was a big, bolshy man and he arrived in a 4x4. I asked him, 'Where's your wife?'. He said she was in the car. I asked him what she was doing. He said, 'Knitting'. Well, I wasn't going to sell the puppy to someone who wasn't even interested enough to get out of the car and come and have a look at it! Anyway, we were in the kitchen, chatting, and I offered to make him a cup of tea. I put the kettle on. I was one end of the kitchen unit and he was further along.

In the corner, by the side of me, are two wooden shelves about fourteen inches long. We keep three tins on the top one, tea, sugar and coffee. They are perfectly secure and I often take them off and polish them. Suddenly the shelf flew across the worktop and knocked the boiling kettle off, all over the man's feet. He never said a word. Afterwards I looked at the rawlplugs and they were still in the wall, the screws had shot out with the shelf. If there had been something wrong with rawlplugs the wall would have been damaged. It was very scary at the time. It was the sort of thing you would like to see in one of those *Haunted House* programmes.

Something unbelievable happened a couple of years ago. We had a large dog, a Rotweiller. He was ten years old. After he passed away we kept seeing a shadow come in through the one side of the back door. It was just a dark shape, you couldn't see any detail, it was about half the size of a man. You know they say that you can see things out of the corner of your eye – well, that was it. Sometimes, I'm sitting in the living room with my son and I say, 'The shadow's with us again'.

A few weeks after my mother-in-law had died, I was lying on my side in bed about two o'clock in the morning, trying to get to sleep when all of a sudden, something sat on the side of the bed and the bed went down. I felt that it was my mother-in-law. I couldn't move and I tried to turn over to get a good look at this person but I couldn't move at all, not even my eyes, I was totally paralysed. In my mind I knew it was her and that she was looking across me at her son. I felt that she was saying, 'I have come for the last time to see if he is OK'. She went after a few minutes but it felt like hours. Funnily enough, I wasn't really scared. (Her husband said that he has felt his mother several times. It terrifies him. His mother was a big woman and so the bed rolls when she sits on it. He dives under the bedclothes).

We see my father quite a lot. My son had my father's bed. I didn't really agree with it but it was a good bed and my son wanted it, so we had it after my father died. I came up the stairs one night and didn't bother to turn on the stairs' lights but in the half-darkness I could clearly see my father sitting on his bed. He had his clothes on, but not his slippers, that was very unusual as he always wore his slippers.

My father was descended from the Romany gypsies. I can see things before they happen. I just can't explain it. When my son was about 14 he had a BMX bike. I'm terrible about bikes and he refused to wear a crash helmet. I kept dreaming he was going to go under a car. He hadn't had the bike long when I went out shopping and when I came back the police were at the door. He had gone up to the shops and a car had knocked him off sideways. He wasn't seriously hurt but he was in hospital for a couple of days.

The Helpful Entity – Worcester Cathedral

Stonemason Oliver Webb has been working on historic buildings throughout the Midlands and has a collection of fascinating stories. Here he tells one from Worcester Cathedral, near to the very spot where Charles Stuart stood to watch the battle:

During my years as a stone mason I inevitably came into contact with hundreds of people in the course of a year and very often people would have "experiences" to relate. One of my favourites came from a chap I used to work with in 1978-79 called Steve. His younger brother (name now long forgotten by me, but call him Bob for the sake of convenience) was an apprentice electrician who had been working, with a mate, Dave, in Worcester Cathedral, wedged in some dark and poky little nook far from the public's gaze. Dave was jammed head first into this nightmarishly inaccessible place trying to perform

"Well you were here just now" said Dave, "because you passed me the drill and the torch". Bob knew full well that he hadn't and that nobody else was in the vicinity. It transpired that somebody unknown had been passing tools silently over Dave's shoulder as he asked for them all the while that Bob was absent.

13

some electrical feat, whilst Bob was just behind him passing tools to him over his shoulder as he asked for them - there being no room for tools where Dave was working. The place was evidently extremely cramped, hot and awkward and the job difficult since they were there for quite a long time. Conversation had apparently dwindled to "More cable", "Big cutters", "Phillip's screwdriver", "Hammer" type of thing and the mood wasn't good.

Bob, getting bored and stiff, eventually decided to have a break and discretely shuffled backwards out of the hole and took a breather in the fresh air - if Dave shouted, he'd soon be back in the hole. Minutes went by and no shout came from the depths so Bob wandered off to the loo and got side-tracked at the van for a cup of tea along the way and so on. Eventually, feeling rather guilty at abandoning Dave for so long in such a horrid place he went back fully expecting an earful from his mate. Scrambling back down into the hole Bob called something along the lines of "I'm back", much to the confusion of Dave who said something along the lines of "Why, where did you go?". There ensued a moment of confusion. "Well you were here just now" said Dave, "because you passed me the drill and the torch". Bob

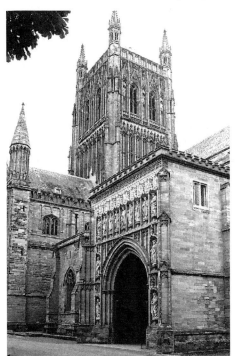

knew full well that he hadn't and that nobody else was in the vicinity. It transpired that somebody unknown had been passing tools silently over Dave's shoulder as he asked for them all the while that Bob was absent.

Unfortunately, far from assisting the job, it had the opposite effect, since Dave scrambled out of that hole and refused to get back in at any price! Someone else had to finish the job. Although I had the story second hand from Steve, he knew Dave and apparently the poor fellow was shaken rigid by the whole episode.

Charles watched the battle from the tower of Worcester Cathedral.

The Cathedral is thought to be haunted by the ghost of Thomas Morris. His grave is marked by the flagstone outside the gift shop which bears the one word – MISERRIMUS (Oh miserable one). He was Vicar of Claines and a minor canon at the Cathedral and, in the 1600s, he refused to swear an Oath of Allegiance to either James II or his successors, William and Mary. Consequently he was never promoted and he stated that, as he had been walked over in life, so he wished to be walked over in death. His ghost has been seen several times and was so well known that, in the days when young policemen were sent to look round the Cathedral at night, the more experienced police officers would hang a coat on the Miserimus door to fall down and terrify their raw colleague.

Hullo and Goodbye - Barbourne

The Barbourne Road runs northward from Worcester, parallel to the Pitchcroft race course, where the Scottish General, Leslie, stood with the cavalry of the Scot army and never joined in the fighting.

David, who tells the next story, still lives in Worcester and has now retired after a successful career:

During the 1950s I lived in one of a row of terraced houses in Lansdowne Street, Barbourne. The houses were divided by an entry, you had to go down the entry and through a little gate to get to your house. We lived one side of the entry and Mr Bayley lived the other side. He was elderly, of medium height and very thin with grey hair.

I was about eleven years of age and I had the back bedroom. My bed was by the window so that I could look out while I was in bed. One evening, I looked through the bedroom window and I remember that it was dark, but I could clearly see Mr Bayley come out of his back door and open the gate. I can still remember his grey hair going up the entry. I thought it was strange because he had been ill for some time.

When I went down to breakfast the next morning I told my mother that I had seen Mr Bayley. She said, 'Well, I don't think so, dear because Mr Bayley passed away last night'.

That's the only paranormal experience I have ever had. It was very odd. It seemed very real to me.

The houses are still there. I sometimes take a nostalgic drive past.

The lovely Tudor House in Friar Street, now run by the Worcester Heritage Amenity Trust.

Nightmares at Tudor House (Friar Street)

One of the most picturesque buildings in Worcester is Tudor House, Friar Street, thought to have been built between 1500 and 1550. Over the last five centuries the building has been a work place for weavers, clothiers, tailors, bakers, painters, and brewers. It has been used as sub-let lodgings, an inn known as the Cross Keys, a tearoom and coffee room, a school clinic (from 1921 to 1971), a World War two air raid wardens post and billet office.

In 1971 the house was taken over by Worcester City Museums service and known as Tudor House Museum, then the Museum of Local Life. It closed to the public in 2003. However, a group of volunteers, known as the Worcester Heritage Amenity Trust, are managing this lovely property and have currently opened it to the public on Wednesdays and Saturdays. For more details contact Helen Wallis on 01905 759344 or manager@ tudorhouse.org.uk.

On a Local Author's Day on 28 April 2007, the Artist in Residence, Maureen, was carrying a pot of water up the stairs, when:

> to my surprise, it suddenly lifted itself out of my hand and dropped on to the floor. I couldn't understand how it happened. The kitchen volunteers were not pleased and I was upbraided.

16

So many strange things have happened since the Trust have taken over that, on Halloween 2006, a paranormal society was invited to spend the night there. A member of the Society was a young lady, Helen, who is also a volunteer at Tudor House, and she reports:

Whilst at Tudor House, the atmosphere didn't give off the friendly welcoming feeling that I am used to. We walked around downstairs first of all, through the coffee room and into the weaving room and while we were there, both my friend and I were drawn to going down into the cellar. We opened the door and took some photos and I decided to sit on a ledge. Suddenly I could hear women shouting and screaming and I could see something swinging from the right hand corner of my eye. I glanced over and saw a young man swinging from the beams. It was at that moment I felt uncomfortable being down there and decided to make a hasty get away from the cellar with the rest of the group following me.

About six months later we had an electrician come in the building and he went into the same cellar. He came out a bit white and said to one of the volunteers, 'There's a lot of sadness down in that cellar'.

Communications from Another World

The Trinity Ladies Group of Worcester very kindly appealed for tales of the inexplicable and two members came forward. The first story is from Mildred who is in her nineties:

My mother was quite distraught after my father died and went away to Oxford to stay with my brother for the weekend. On the Saturday, I went out and it was very strange coming home to an empty house. I went to bed and something woke me up. My mother had those lace curtains and the moonlight was streaming in through the window. I looked at the clock and it was a quarter to twelve. Then I saw that there was a man standing by the window. At first I thought it was one of my brothers, larking about. Because of the light coming in from the window I could only see a silhouette but it was definitely my father. He was a very big man and had a very large head, his silhouette was unmistakable. Later, I told my brother and his reply was, 'You are stupid, you must have been dreaming'.

There was no telephone in those days and a day or two later I had a letter from my mother, saying she would be staying on in Oxford as she had been taken very ill on the Saturday. It was just as if my dad was trying to tell me that she was poorly. It was very peculiar.

Mildred's friend, Betty says that when she was young, she was a shocker to get up in the morning:

My mother would call and call me, but I wouldn't get up. Some mornings I would push it a lot and she would swear at me. She would put her head round the door and say, 'Are you getting out of that so-and-so bed?'. Even when I was a little girl at school she would swear at me.

Then, when I was 30, my mother died in hospital. Every morning for a week after, when I was in bed, her head would come round the door. It didn't bother me. I just thought, 'Oh, I had better get up now or I shall be late for work'.

Visitors in the Severn Traveller

The Worcester and Birmingham Canal joins the river Severn on the southern side of the town, at Diglis. A walk southwards along the river, past the Cathedral, will bring you to the Diglis Locks, constructed chiefly in the 1840s.

There are not many steamer skippers left, but Ernie is one of them and he has a strange tale to tell about one of the boats.

The Severn Traveller was originally a tanker which used to go up and down the Severn in the 1930's, usually between Stourport and Sharpness. Then she overturned in the channel when she was at anchor. There might have been some fatalities.

When the tanker finished she was carrying stone for a channel-based company. They took the top off her, she was just an open boat so that they could throw the stone in. Finally, they beached her on the bank. About forty years ago, my boss, Norman Dawson, bought her.

Dawson was boat mad. There was a boat repair company, Everton's, of Diglis Basin in Worcester, they had been there for years. They had a boat repair yard and ran steamers from there. Dawson bought them out.

When he had first bought the Traveller from Sharpness, and was bringing her upstream to the Diglis Basin in Worcester, he drew a design on the back of a cigarette packet and pinned it on the wall. He said, 'That's how I want her to look'. He changed her into a steamer and converted her into a pleasure boat. We did the river boat shuffles with a disco on board, I went to Tewkesbury several times. I remember the first time we took her out, the ladies were all dancing in their long white dresses and the paint wasn't quite dry so they got paint on them.

Photograph of the Severn Traveller, taken from River Severn Passenger 'Steamers 1956-1986', *by Len Holder.*

Dawson never had any big ideas, he was just content with his yard and his steamers. He lived at Kempsey, next to the river. He was getting on in years and was taken ill several times, eventually, he died.

One night, I was going down past Kempsey in the Severn Traveller. She had a big, broad wheelhouse with doors on both sides. That night, there was no wind and the windows were closed. As we were going past the slip where Dawson used to be, both doors slammed at the same time, and inside the wheelhouse it went freezing cold. Logically, it was impossible for two doors to bang at the same time.

Several times we would sit down with a half of beer after the trip and we would hear footsteps on the decks. I would think that someone had climbed on to the steamer and go and have a look but no-one would be there.

The crew didn't like going downstairs and one crewman, Paul Bellamy, flatly refused to go down.

We always said Norman Dawson was on that boat.

The Haunted Bus

Jill now lives in Northwick but in 1949, she was living in Kent, in an estate cottage belonging to Oxney Court.

The Court itself was, at that time, in ruins. It was very remote, a long drive went up to the old manse house with woods on either side. We were serviced by an hourly bus, and on a Saturday night I often went dancing with two of my friends, to either Ringwold or Deal. One Saturday night we decided not to go dancing and to have a night in, and we all stayed at our respective homes for the whole evening.

We heard later that the bus had seen a figure at the bus stop at our usual time so the bus had stopped. The conductress and the conductor were not taking much notice of the passenger because the conductress was leaning through the little hatch into the driving compartment that they had in those days, and talking to the driver. They both heard footsteps clattering up the stairs. However, when the conductress went upstairs to take the fare, nobody was there.

After that, the conductor and conductress refused to do a night shift.

The Haunted Holiday

Dennis and his wife Jessie live near Worcester and about 20 years ago decided to have a late walking holiday at the end of October, in Llanfairfechan, near Bangor, on the Welsh coast.

We stayed in an old house which was a cross between a hostel and a hotel – a large Victorian house up a drive. It must have been built by some coal magnate and had been converted into a holiday complex. It was the end of the season and we were the last people staying there. The warden, his wife and family were still in residence, we went down and had a meal with them. It was all very friendly.

As it got dark early, after dinner we went and played table tennis. Whist we were playing a door opened behind us for no reason. We went out to see what was going on. Nobody was there. We didn't think twice about it and just gave the door a good push to make sure it was absolutely closed. The same thing happened again. We rushed to the door and looked up the stairs. Not a soul was about. We were a bit unsettled but we went on playing, we thought it was just one of those things.

Eventually we decided to turn in for the night. Our room was on the top floor, at the end of a longish corridor. We were very comfortable and we settled down for the night. We hadn't long been asleep when we heard somebody come into the room next to us. It sounded as if they were unpacking things. We could hear them quite plainly. We could hear them walking about, drawers were opening and closing and the wardrobe doors were banging open and shut. We just said, 'Some people are very inconsiderate. They have no sympathy for others'. When they had quietened down we went back to sleep.

The next morning we noticed the door to the bedroom next door was open and, being a bit nosey, we looked in as we walked past. It was quite empty. There was no furniture in there, nothing. We felt a bit put out, in fact we felt quite upset. We decided that when somebody came down to breakfast we would ask them who came in during the night. We would mention politely that we heard them come in.

When the warden came into breakfast we said, 'Who came into the room next to ours last night then?'. She said that nobody came in. We told her that we had heard someone come in and they were unpacking. She said, 'Oh dear, we have heard this sort of thing happening before. We can't explain it either. We just know there is something going on but we don't know what it is'. There was no-one else in the house at all, it was a still night and there were no street noises as the house was up its own drive.

We were only booked in for the one night so we didn't stay there again. Nothing like that has happened to us before or since.

A Slip in Time

One of the first tales in this chapter was about Worcester Cathedral by the Worcestershire stonemason, Oliver Webb. He has persuaded his friend Alan, to email us about a disappearing shop in Wales:

It was a cold, dark morning in the middle of June and I was working in Wales. You can appreciate the fact that it can be gloomy in the Welsh hills. I had been restoring an old barn for a neighbour who had a holiday cottage where he rested from farming.

He asked me to do some renovations to the house and in particular replace a couple of windows. I had contacted a carpenter in Builth and he had phoned advising that the windows could be collected. Peter, the owner possessed a "school" clock and kept mentioning to me that, should I go to Builth, perhaps I could enquire about having it fixed.

As I travelled down the High Street there is a road at the end which bends to the right to go to Llanwrtyd Wells and also turns sharp to the left and climbs the hill. On turning to the left I noticed a store which was open and the sign read "olde clocks repaired". The shop was painted green and there was decorative leafwork painted around the door portals.

How convenient, I would call in after picking up the windows and check them out on the repair of Peter's clock. Having loaded the windows into the A35 van I asked the carpenter his thoughts on the store at the intersection, whether he could recommend me taking the clock there to be repaired. "What store?" he replied. I felt he must be rather unobservant since he must see the shop as he came down to the junction - it was facing him directly. I described the clock shop to him and after further frustration realised that we were getting nowhere.

I travelled down the hill and came to the junction and there wasn't a clock shop to be seen. I was so dumbfounded that I left the A35 van and went into the current store which was selling bread and cakes; they were quite puzzled as I asked them where the clock shop had gone. Only 30 minutes prior I had seen the store with its door open for business!

When I arrived back at the place where I normally left the van, I met Dick, the old farmer, and related the tale and he then informed me that my description of the store front was indeed accurate except that it had closed for business 20 years earlier … I always wonder what would have happened if I had gone in initially, as I was tempted to do on first seeing the shop to make enquiries, but then thought that I would pick-up the windows first!!

There we go.....I'm not psychic, but it is mysterious to say the least!

The old Butter Street runs along the side of St Nicholas Church.

A few years ago we had a friend who lived in a house across the road from the old school. We were very upset for him when his wife, Marie* died from cancer and we went to the funeral. I remember that it was a beautiful summer's day, and really warm.

When the funeral was over three of us were invited back to the house for food and drink so we started walking back towards the house from Alcester Church. A lady was walking towards us in a bright red and orange oriental-style dress looking just like Marie and as she was walking she seemed to be rinsing her hands, wringing them first one way, then the other. She carried on up towards the church. When we reached my friend's house, I said to him, 'Marie's sister is a dead ringer of her'. He said, 'Marie hasn't got a sister'.

When we discussed it later, it seemed that two of us saw the lady but one didn't. But the more you think about it, the more strange it seems. Would someone be going to a funeral in a vivid red and orange dress? She was as solid as you and me.

Leave Me Alone!

When they go to bed at night, people often feel that someone is sitting or walking on the bed, or holding them down. Parapsychologists say that there is a state halfway between sleeping and waking where events seem real but are actually in a dream. This may explain some but not all of the experiences:

I came to live in Alcester and for the first six months I was in a house that dated back to the 16th century. I used to watch the telly downstairs and I would very often go to sleep on the sofa, then wake up and take myself off to bed. One night, I had fallen asleep and I had pulled a cover over myself. I woke up and, half asleep, I felt that someone was pushing down on the side of me. I couldn't speak, I couldn't do anything, I was like – paralysed. Then something pressed down on me again. I was suddenly wide awake. I looked up but I couldn't see anything. I felt it pressing down on me again and that time I found my voice and I screamed. I turned onto my side so that I had my back towards the entity and, do you know, it had the cheek to press down on me again. I shouted, 'Leave me alone', and nothing happened after that. I have now lived in Alcester for many years and have not had another experience since.

A Holy Ghost

In an obscure history book in Redditch library is a note concerning Beoley Church, 'Parson Gittins was much troubled by the ghost of his predecessor'. Evidently his predecessor returned regularly to take the eucharist. Here is a similar tale, told by Marjorie at a meeting in Alcester. Unfortunately, her husband has now passed away and she can't remember the church, only that it was just over the border in Worcestershire. It sounds as if it's a Roman Catholic church. If anyone knows the name of the church and the full story, we would love to hear it.

My husband saw a ghost in a church. He was minding the Eucharist and all of a sudden the apparition of a priest appeared on his right, genuflexed as though he was doing communion and then disappeared on his other side. My husband was a bit perturbed at the time and wondered what the heck he was. So he asked the priest the next day who said, 'Oh yes, he was giving a funeral, he dropped dead right in front of the altar and often when we have a funeral or a communion he is there. It's very annoying because he frightens people, did he frighten you?'. My husband said, 'No, I just wondered what the heck he was, that's all, and where he came from'. The priest said, 'Yes, it's a young priest that just happened to have a heart attack as he was taking a funeral.'

BROMSGROVE

t the time of the Domesday Survey in 1086 this pleasant market town had a population of about 100. It became famous for its cloths and, when this trade declined in the 1800s, for nail-making. Overlooking the town is the Perpendicular tower of St Peter's, rising to 200 feet. Bromsgrove has a famous school, founded in the sixteenth century. Among its pupils was the poet, AE Housman, who, it is said, has sold more books of poetry than any other English poet. His father had a solicitor's practice at Perry Hall and a statue of the poet graces the centre of the town.

Bromsgrove is also famous for playing a part in the flight of Charles Stuart (the future Charles II) from the Battle of Worcester.

Charles Stuart was extremely lucky to escape from the Battle of Worcester. He was easily recognisable, being over six feet tall and having a swarthy complexion. A large contingent of soldiers rode with him, these were chiefly General Leslie's cavalry who had refused to join in the battle. Charles complained that he could not get them to fight for him, now he could not get rid of them! They rode through Ombersley to Hartlebury until they reached the Kidderminster Road. In order to make good his escape, Charles had to get rid of them, so while the other fugitives carried on to Kidderminster, Charles, together with the Duke of Buckingham and a few others, turned off and rode through Chaddesley Corbett, Hagley and Pedmore to Stourbridge.

After they had been riding for less than two hours, disaster struck. Charles' horse threw a shoe. The small party urgently needed a quiet blacksmith where no questions would be asked. At that time Ye Olde Black Cross, in Bromsgrove, was not a pub but a small blacksmiths on the main road from Worcester and many historians agree that this is where Charles went to have his horse shod. In later years, this was one of Charles' favourite anecdotes which he told as follows:

We took our journey towards Bristol, resolving to lie at a place called Long Marston in the Vale of Evesham. We had not gone two hours on our way before the mare I rode cast a shoe, so we were forced to ride to get another shoe at a scattering village, whose name began with something like 'Long-' and as I was holding my horses' foot, I asked the smith the news. He told there was no news that he knew of, since the good news of the beatings of the rogues, the Scots. I asked him whether there were none of the English taken that joined with the Scots. He answered that he did not hear that rogue, Charles Stuart, was taken, but some of the others, he said, were taken, but not

Charles Stuart. I told him if that rogue were taken he deserved to be hanged more than all the rest for bringing in the Scots, upon which he said I spoke like an honest man, and we parted.

Cavaliers in the Ladies' Loo

Ye Olde Black Cross is still there with a glass-covered hole in the floor, so that you should be able to peep down and see the rings in the wall where Charles tethered his horse, but unfortunately the glass has become so scratched it's now difficult to see through it.

The staff have had many strange experiences. Reg and Edith Jackson Cox were the licencees from 1970 to 1983 and Reg said that there were several visitations. A female supervisor came face to face with a Cavalier in the ladies' loos. An Assistant Manager was in bed when a figure appeared and walked through the door. There were all kinds of weird noises and creaks, for example, one evening Reg was sitting in the lounge when he heard a tremendous crash. His wife was ill and he thought she had fallen out of bed but she hadn't moved.

The present bartender, Dave, has now been working at the inn for about a year, and says:

I live with my partner in the first floor flat and we often hear footsteps coming up the stairs. When we first moved in, we didn't have a lock on the door. Early one morning, I was in the shower and my girlfriend was still in bed when she heard footsteps coming up the stairs and towards the bedroom door. The latch of the door lifted and the door opened. She put her head out over the blankets to see who had come in but nobody was there. After that, we had a lock fitted.

The Black Cross

When I've finished at night I usually sit downstairs in the bar and have a drink. About half-past three early one morning my partner came running down the stairs to fetch me. She had felt the bed being depressed on one side as if someone was sitting on it.

Only this morning, when we got up my girlfriend send to me, 'Did you go out of the room at all last night while I was asleep because this morning the latch was off?'. I said that I hadn't gone anywhere. Twenty minutes later she came out of the bathroom and said, 'Have you just been out?'. 'No, I haven't'. 'Well, the latch is off again'.

The Ghosts of Grafton Manor

In St Peter's huge graveyard are two decorative monuments often photographed by train enthusiasts. They are to Thomas Scaife and Joseph Rutherford, two engineers (probably engine drivers) killed in 1840 by an exploding boiler of a Birmingham and Gloucester railway engine. Less accessible in these days of locked churches is a monument to the owner of Grafton Manor, Sir Humphrey Stafford, who died more than 550 years ago, in 1450, when Grafton was a larger village than Bromsgrove. Sir Humphrey and his brother were killed fighting Jack Cade and his rebels at Sevenoaks in Kent. The rebels were not outlaws and down-and-outs but the local gentry. The yeomen and the smaller landed proprietors of Kent and Sussex were furious at the levels of taxation and waste of money by Henry VI and his advisers. Led by Jack Cade, they marched towards London, overcoming the king's troops at Sevenoaks, and stormed into the city. The mayor stopped them by closing London bridge. They sent for the Chancellor of the Exchequer and had him beheaded at Cheapside. Negotiations between the archbishop and Cade resulted in the rebels agreeing to return home.

Sir Humphrey's son also met a tragic end. He fought for Richard III at the Battle of Bosworth in 1485 against Henry, Earl of Richmond. Richard III was killed and Henry became Henry VII. Sir Humphrey's son survived the battle, only to be executed for high treason. Therefore, in the second half of the 1400s, two owners of Grafton Manor met a violent death.

One of the generals of the opposing army was Sir Gilbert Talbot, and the ownership of Grafton Manor passed to him. He married twice, his first wife was a wealthy widow, and by his second wife he bore a son, John, who also married twice. John's effigy assumed great importance when Lord Talbot was trying to prove a claim as Earl of Shrewsbury. No relevant paperwork could be found but, on cleaning the inscription, evidence was found to link Lord Talbot with the Shrewsbury aristocrats. The Talbots were ardent

Grafton Manor Lake

Royalists and Catholics. Sir Gilbert Talbot's great grandson was John Talbot who, as a Roman Catholic, spent most of his life either in prison or under curfew in or around London. In 1588 he was allowed to return to Grafton on account of the 'longe sickness and indisposicion' of his wife but he was not set at liberty for another ten years.

Towards the end of the Civil War, in 1645, the Talbots were in Worcester, helping in the defence of the town.

Hell for Leather

The house was extensively redeveloped in the 1860s and is now a hotel. The history of Grafton Manor provides a whole series of grieving widows, perhaps one of these is the traditional white lady that floats across the romantic-looking pool in the grounds of Grafton Manor. The ghost has been seen innumerable times over the years, for example, in 1995, by two young couples. Carl Mills said at the time:

> We noticed, through a gap in the hedge on the left, a patch of fog on the bank. It was most peculiar fog and kept rolling off the bank and dropping into the water. Suddenly, it came towards us and when it was ten or fifteen feet away it started to swirl in two spirals, perfect circles, side by side, both going in opposite directions, rather like candy floss. When it was about 10 or 15 feet away the shape began to change and it began to assume human form. It went up and up until it was about six feet tall and at the same time it narrowed, so that it was very thin. The top part seemed to divide into two peaks like arms. When it came to within six feet of us we decided to retreat to the car.

Elwyn Porter adds his name to the list of those who have been privileged enough to see the Grafton ghost, although the traditional apparition seems to have gone through a sex change::

Forty-two years ago I was a young lad of 18 and for about eighteen months I was in a gang of a dozen or so lads. We used to go out on our motor bikes.

I have a suspicion that it was Hallowe'en, that's why we wanted to find a ghost, but anyway, one night in late October, seven or eight of us set off to find the traditional white lady of Grafton Pool. We parked our bikes at the top of the lane adjacent to the A38, about a mile away from Grafton Manor.

We were just messing about as eighteen year olds do, just killing time, this was before the days of the motorways and there weren't many places to go to and there wasn't much to do. We were perfectly sober – we hadn't been drinking as we were going out on our bikes. Grafton manor is privately owned, we knew that we were trespassing so we walked down on the inside of the hedgerow. We went on a bit, conversing and laughing and joking, then, as there was nothing unusual to be seen, we walked back up through the cemetery. It must have been about one o'clock. Then, by the light of the moon we saw, coming towards us, a dark figure. As we were trespassing, we ducked down behind various headstones. I could make out that he was tall and slim and very elegant, very upright. He had a black coat that came down to the top of his calf, I'm not into historical costumes but I would say that he was Edwardian. I think that he had grey hair curling at the collar but I only saw him by moonlight and 42 years have elapsed since then! He took no notice of us and seemed preoccupied, looking straight forward. There was no doubt that he was a person and he was very real. He seemed to be drifting, rather than walking. He went between the first two gravestones but when it came to the next two, he went straight through them. I've no idea what happened after that because we turned tail and ran all the way back to the bikes, eight large lads tearing through Grafton hell for leather. When we got back to our bikes we conferred and agreed that we had all seen the same thing.

I have lost touch with everyone now, but if one of the lads reads this and recognises my name, he will confirm my story.

Please note that Grafton pool is on private property.

Precognition – or What?

Parapsychologists give interesting insights into the world of the inexplicable. George Gregg is such a person and a member of Parasearch, a Midland group who investigate ghosts, hauntings and other paranormal activities. George has had various strange experiences himself and so he can observe these happenings both as a participant and a psychologist. Here he gives two explanations for a personal incident, a paranormal and a psychological one:

In 1984 I caught a bus into Bromsgrove in order to pay a few bills and do a few domestic errands. I was due at work at about 12.00 midday. I was working at a local Mental Health Unit in my role as Registered Mental Health Nurse. My house is one stop before the Unit.

I jumped back on to the bus with all the intention of going straight to work. I'm the kind of person who is conscientious and hated being late for work. Nevertheless, as the bus was approaching the stop near my house, I got a strange urge to get off the bus and go home. I jumped off the bus at the stop before my intended one which is only a few yards from home.

As I arrived home I could see smoke in my living room. I opened the front door pulled out my handkerchief and followed the source of the smoke which turned out to be the electric cooker. Apparently what had happened was that morning the toaster had broken, so my wife used the grill pan to do the toast but forgot all about it.

I arrived just as the pan had caught fire. I grabbed the grill pan as flames were rising up through the top of the cooker and threw it into the back garden. I then looked around the house for my wife and 18 month old daughter. They were both in the bath, oblivious to the danger they were in.

I am convinced if I hadn't got home when I did they would not be alive today.

Paranormal Explanation: Either precognition (seeing the future) or clairvoyance (I perceived the cooker was about to set on fire outside my five senses, ESP?)

Psychological Explanation: Coincidence, I was feeling vaguely unwell, after all there was no voice saying to me: 'George go home, your cookers ablaze'. Or it could have been anxiety, at some level, based upon the knowledge that the toaster was broken?

A Clip Round the Ear'ole

We hope this book will convince parents that children do see ghosts, and that it will save future generations from 'a clip round the ear'ole'.

A friend of mine lives in a Victorian house in Bromsgrove. She has a poltergeist which seems to be seasonal, for some months nothing happens and then it will start up again. She is very fussy about locking the doors and switching off the lights before she goes to bed, but

31

The well-known poet, Alfred E Housman, stands guard over Bromsgrove High Street. He was born near Bromsgrove and educated at Bromsgrove School.

when she gets up in the morning the lights are on and the doors are unlocked. Also, she will be talking to her husband and all of a sudden her voice starts to echo as if she's speaking in an empty church.

It's the family home, her parents were there before her and she lived there as a little girl. They were a large family and all the kiddies slept in one bed. She woke up one night to see a woman standing over her. When she got up in the morning she said to her mother 'There was a lady looking over me in the night' but she just got a clip round the ear 'ole for telling lies. Then her mum was speaking to one of the neighbours who recognised the ghost from the child's description. She said that it was a lady who lived there previously and she comes back to look after the children.

DROITWICH

ny introduction to Droitwich must refer to the salt trade. The town is sitting on a huge underground reservoir of salt water and was once the great salt town of the Midlands. The brine was said to be 12 times stronger than sea water and 40% more dense than the Red Sea. Up until about 100 years ago, salt was one of the basic necessities of life. As well as its current use for flavouring, it was widely used as an antiseptic and before the days of fridges it was indispensable as a preservative. The Romans lost no time in appropriating the lucrative town of white gold and Roman roads from Droitwich radiated out all over England. So much salt water was taken out from underground that the middle of the High Street dropped in the centre and had to be rebuilt. Even now the houses there tend to lean slightly.

If you are visiting Droitwich, do go to the Council's One-Stop Shop and have a look at the two medieval dolls displayed in the glass case. They were discovered in the walls of the house in 1996 by Council workmen. Historians identified them as 'good luck' dolls. They were whisked off to the County Museum but as soon as they went, bad luck hit the workmen. A digger ploughed through a power cable, ancient foundations were discovered and work was stopped. A 'flu epidemic halted work again, followed by a spell of atrocious weather. The workmen asked for the dolls to be put back into the premises and there they sit to this day.

The tale is told that Saint Richard saved the salt mines in the early 1200s. He is said to have been born in Droitwich on the site of the Raven Hotel, to have been educated at Oxford but returned home to rebuild the family fortunes. He was elected Bishop of Chichester but the King refused to let him take up the post as he wanted someone else to be appointed, so Saint Richard became a homeless wanderer. When, in later years, he visited the town, the brine springs had dried up and consequently, so had the town's income. Saint Richard blessed the springs and they flowed again. The bailiff cried 'My Lord, you have saved the town, let this day never be forgotten! In case Droitwich folk have forgotten, it was 3rd April.

If you park in the main car park by Waitrose, most of the salt mines were over the other side of the road, known as The Saltway. One of the salt mines, a deep well, has been preserved. If you look up, you will see above you the great church of St Augustines at Dodderhill, towering over the river Salwarpe. This is where the cannon was placed during the earlier Civil War that blew Friar Street apart.

From May the 11th to 14th 1645 the king himself, Charles 1 stayed here with his regiment of foot and horse. At the end of Friar Street was a church where

the Royalists kept their ammunition. The supply had originally belonged to the Parliamentarians but had been captured by the Royalists. No doubt the Parliamentarians wanted to get their own back, and so they brought a cannon to Dodderhill and fired down on the town. The church was blasted away, so much so that only three windows and a stone carving of a head are known to have survived which have been incorporated into the Old Cock Inn, halfway down Friar Street.

Beauty and the Bakers

The next two narratives have been given by two local gentlemen who attended a meeting of the Droitwich Probus Club in September 2006:

In Newlands, which is just south of Droitwich, there was a bakehouse that had been owned by the same family for three or four generations. I think the building went back to the 1600s. They supplied bread right across the Droitwich area. My wife was related to them so we often went to visit.

The toilet was at the bottom of the garden. One lovely moonlit night – it must have been in the autumn of about 1976 – I went out to the toilet and strolled down the path. It was a beautiful night with one of the harvest moons. As I walked down the path a lady came out of the toilet. Her dress was black and I think it was made of lace, it was floor length, quite loose-fitting and with buttons down the front. She had black hair, she was about 5 feet 9 inches tall and she was wearing a red rose. She passed me about two feet away on the right-hand side and as she went by she looked at me and smiled sweetly. She was such a charming lady. I said, 'Good evening' or something like that. She never said anything but she had a lovely smile.

I came back into the house and said to Peggy, our relative, 'Who was the lady that I have just seen?'. She said, 'Oh, that's my great, great grandmother'. She opened a drawer, got a photograph out and there was the lady I had just seen. Peggy told me that she had been around before, several

Dodderhill Church towering over the town. The Parliamentarians placed a cannon here and blasted the town. The tower was rebuilt in 1708.

The Old Cock Inn, evidently rebuilt after the Civil War incorporating parts from a destroyed church.

people had seen her. I saw her as plain as anything. I had had a glass of wine but I wasn't that far gone!

I was taken aback but I found it quite fascinating. I was pleased that I had seen a ghost. Whenever I went on a visit to the bakery I hoped to see the ghost again. Perhaps, if it had been a man waving a stick I might have felt differently!

The Black Pudding Apparition

Although the next ghost was seen in Huddersfield, the gentleman concerned lives in Droitwich and we felt that we must include it as it is such an entertaining tale. If anyone else has had a strange experience after eating black pudding we would love to hear about it.

Round about 1977 I was working for the local authority as Head of IT and, although I was living in Droitwich, I was working all round the country. I usually stayed there during the week and came home at weekends.

For some weeks I stayed at a b&b in Huddersfield, in a very old building, I would say Victorian – nineteenth century. It was a huge place. One morning, at about 7 am, I went down early to the breakfast room and sat there eating my breakfast. I was the only one in the room. I was just tucking into black pudding when a Victorian lady appeared in the corner where the cereals were on a table for your breakfast. She just appeared from nowhere. She was middle-aged and wearing a long brown dress that came down the floor and stuck out at the back, I suppose you would call it a bustle, and a high collar. Her hair was greyish and long, just hanging down. She slowly glided across the side of the room to the left then went through an open doorway and disappeared. I watched her for several seconds. She was solid and yet she didn't seem quite solid – it's difficult to explain.

That's the only time I have ever seen a ghost. My reaction was one of surprise. I didn't mention it to anyone – afterwards I blamed it on the black pudding!

A House-Proud Entity

Many of our first class stories have been from wives relating their husband's experiences, and here is another one:

My husband, Adam, was working as a driver a couple of years ago, delivering food. He was called, at a late hour of the night, to an address near the junction of the Worcester Road and High Street in Droitwich. He tried the bell to the flat but could get no answer. Realising the front door was slightly ajar, he stepped into the communal hall with the shopping and closed the door behind him. Although the hall was in darkness, the street lighting shone through a broken pane of glass in the front door and he could faintly see loose mail scattered all over the floor. Unfortunately, the timer light switch was on the landing outside the flat so he had to run up the stairs in the dark! Notwithstanding, he left the shopping in the hall, ran up the stairs to switch on the light, then ran back down and took the shopping up. By this time the stairs light had gone out so he quickly put the light on again, knocked on both doors on the landing and, receiving no answer, started back down the stairs. When he reached the bottom of the stairs he saw all of the letters that had been scattered on the floor were now neatly stacked into a pile! There had been no-one around, no-one had

Droitwich High Street. It joins the Worcester Road at the far end. Notice the way the houses dip halfway down the street due to subsidence. The 'One-Stop Shop' containing the 'Good Luck' dolls is near the far end on the right.

come in off the street and he saw nobody from his view at the top of the stairs which was always in sight to him.

Some weeks later he was called to the same address but this time he gained access and the tenants, unprompted, apologised for not being in previously as they didn't like staying in - even for their shopping, because the place was extremely haunted, so much so, that they in fact were moving within a few days.

Jinxed Money Boxes

Ann seems to have a mild poltergeist:

Lights flicker in our house and strange things happen. For example, I did a jigsaw and there was one piece missing. The jigsaw was to be passed on so I wrote on the box, 'one piece missing'. Two days later the missing piece was lying on the mat in the middle of the doorway. This is the only doorway in and out of the house and had been used dozens of times.

My main story starts in September when I went down to Weston. In a shop were some ceramic money boxes - they were a bit like ceramic jam jars. There was a yellow one for girls with a lime green lid and on it was the slogan 'Girls Night Out'. You were supposed to save your money on it to pay for a night out. The boys' money boxes were orange with a blue lid and on it, it said, 'Pub Money'. I thought, 'That's brilliant, I'll buy two for my two girls and two for the two boys'. I carefully stored the girls' to the left and the boys' to the right.

On Christmas afternoon (I work on Christmas morning) my younger son said, in a sarcastic voice, 'Thanks a lot, mum'. I asked him, 'What's the matter?' He held out the box and it said, 'Girls Night Out'. I said, 'Oh bother, I've got them mixed up'. I undid the wrapping round the money box that I'd put for my one daughter and that money box was yellow, a girl's box. I undid the other and that also said, 'Girls Night Out'.

I phoned my other son and asked him to have a look at his money box. and tell me what it said. The answer was, 'Pub Money'. I now had three of one and one of the other. I thought I must have got them mixed up in the shop.

That evening, I said to my younger son, 'Have a look and tell me what it says on the outer cardboard box'. I thought perhaps the wrong money box had been put in the container. The answer was, 'Pub mon-ey'. I said, 'Take it out of the box and see what it says'. The money box also read 'Pub money'. I must admit I was a bit frightened. I thought, 'Am I losing my marbles?'. It did bother me.

The Haunted Family

The Westlands Estate, Droitwich, was originally known as the Boycott Estate. The first houses were only temporary, then new houses were built. The following horrifying story comes from one of the first families to move into the estate. Nearly all the family have been kind enough to talk about their experiences. The father probably suffered most and so we have begun with his version of events

All this happened when we were living in a Council House in Droitwich. My wife wanted to change to a larger house as we had two boys and two girls, and as there was a three-bedroomed house going over the road, we decided to apply for it. The people who lived there were very keen to get out. They did all the running around for us - all the paperwork and so on. At the time we thought it was a bit strange.

It all started happening shortly after we moved. One night I had got out of bed to go to the toilet when I saw a haze on the stairs that seemed to be a figure. The shape was misty and glowing, about four or five feet tall. My daughter came in late and the next morning, when we saw her, she said, 'Last night I had the fright of my life. I came upstairs, there was a light glowing on the stairs and I saw a person there'.

Another night, when everyone was in bed, we heard a terrific crash. It was as if a wardrobe had fallen over, it shook the house. I dashed upstairs but nothing had fallen over. The neighbours on the one side were on holiday and the house on the other side was empty.

I would come home and I would wave to my wife in the bedroom window. Then I would get in the house and she would be in the kitchen. I would say, 'My word, you got down those stairs quickly' and she would say, 'What do you mean? - I haven't been upstairs'. There were loads of instances like that.

My wife died suddenly in that house. Her cousin came to help with the housework and we eventually got together so that she became my present wife.

We had got some friends round - my second wife's dad and mum and others, it was getting towards midnight when suddenly, an ornament leaped off the coffee table and made us all jump. My first wife's mother died that night at exactly the same time. I'm not a believer but there were happenings in that house that I couldn't explain.

We borrowed my mother's dog. My mother wasn't too well and we said, 'We will look after the dog for you'. All the time he was in our house the dog hid behind a chair, he wouldn't come out, yet he was OK when we went out. His behaviour was very strange.

If one thing had happened on its own we would have known there was an explanation but it wasn't like that, lots of little things happened all the time, week in and week out.

A lot of things happened to my present wife. When she was cleaning in the first floor bedroom, she picked up some rubbish, bits of paper and so on, and pushed it in an empty wine bottle. She threw it into the lounge intending to take it out with the rubbish (the lounge was on the first floor) but it didn't drop, it floated along and floated down the stairs.

Another time she was doing some ironing when she saw a vase of flowers tip over on to its side and back up again.

I'm an electrical engineer by trade and I built a device on the landing that detected any build-up of static. The first person to set it off was one of my daughters, who came back late, as usual, and took off a woollen cardigan as she was going up the stairs. That's full of static. It didn't go off any other time but the readings were astronomical. I can't remember what they were but I know they were extremely high.

For several years I was a Field Engineer for Radio Rentals. I went on a visit to a public house in Stourport-on-Severn, and who should be living there but the people who had the house before us. I said to the husband, 'You know when you were in our house, did anything strange happen?'. His face changed completely. He said, 'I think you had better come into the back room' and he found somebody else to look after the bar while we went into the kitchen.

He said that before he moved to Droitwich he had a quiet, placid dog but after he moved the dog went mad and ripped the curtains. This happened several times, the dog never settled there. Eventually the wife had a baby. She kept the baby in the first floor lounge while she was working in the kitchen on the ground floor. She had an uneasy feeling so she dashed upstairs to find that the baby had turned blue and stopped breathing. She grabbed the baby and squeezed it, dialled 999, tried mouth to mouth and the baby was rushed into hospital. It recovered, but the hospital couldn't find anything wrong with the baby, nobody knew what had caused it to stop breathing. I'm not sure of the time period, but about two weeks later it happened again. The wife had an uneasy feeling - this time she was checking on the baby every few minutes - and again the baby was rushed into hospital. The baby was kept in hospital for about three weeks. Again, they couldn't find anything wrong with it, it was a normal, healthy baby. About that time they realised there was something not quite right with the house. That's when they decided to move.

We just accepted a lot of the strange events. We did keep a record but unfortunately, when we moved we lost it.

The children are now adult, and one January evening in 2006 Harry*, Ann* and Jeanette* met in a Droitwich pub to talk about their childhood experiences. By way of introduction, Harry remarks:

All of us will have one story or another which will relate to something extraordinary happening there. I still recall how terrified I was. We don't talk about it now but it's always there at the back of our minds. My father and step-mother saw more than we did. My step-mother experienced things moving and jumping off shelves. Once, a plate came flying through the air.

I was six years old when we moved to Droitwich. There always seemed to be a sense of something not quite right in our house. My memories and recollections of things that happened will be far more vague than those of my sister's. It was probably the only time in my life I remember not being able to shout out, I was so scared I was not even able to talk. If anyone now were to tell me that they were that scared, I wouldn't believe him. Things I have seen personally in that house, you wouldn't believe. The one closest to my mind was that I was lying on my bed when a hand appeared round the open bedroom

Part of the Westlands Estate

door, it seemed to be holding on to the edge of the door from behind. That was the point where I was unable to scream. I wanted to call my mother or father but nothing came out of my mouth. I was frozen.'

His eldest sister, Jeanette, adds:

I have also seen a hand. I would have been about twelve, or older. I heard someone calling me, I don't know whether it was real or not as it was a very busy household and we were always calling each other. I went to the foot of the stairs and was looking up the stairs to see who it was and there was the hand on the banister. It was a man's hand, strong and not old, I would say middle-aged.

It was a three-storey house and there were four flights of stairs. We hated those stairs. We never walked down the stairs, we jumped from one flight to another. The stair carpet never got worn out! Nobody used it!

On the top floor was a long landing with two doors, one was my bedroom and the other was my brother's bedroom. I remember that I was on my own on the top floor, I came out of my bedroom and I saw a dark shape step out of my brother's room right in front of me, about two feet away. It was so quick! It was quite a big shape, I wouldn't expect it to be a woman's frame, more a man's and it was black and mist-like, not really solid, I could see through it. I jumped, turned and flew down the stairs. I ran into the kitchen and told my sister and my mum and dad. My sister asked why I was panicking.

Mum was a lovely warm person, very generous, never serious and always laughing. One day mum and dad went out in the car and they had a crash. Neither of them were seriously hurt, although mum had bruised her legs. Mum was wearing a gold necklace with a Tutankhamun pendant. When she took it off there was blood on the back of it, although there was no blood anywhere. She threw it out of the door. Three or four weeks later she had a heart attack and died in the house. She was only in her early forties. It was only after that that the strange things began to happen.'

The younger sister, Ann, says:

The two of us slept in the same bed. I was so scared I couldn't even get up in the night to go to the toilet. If I needed to go in the night it was such an upheaval. First I would wake up Jeanette, who would have to get out of bed and switch on the bedroom, landing and bathroom lights. Then she would have to wait until I had got back to bed, she would turn the lights off and have to wait until my feet were off the ground before she turned the bedroom light off.'

These strange goings-on were not only in our house, I used to babysit for our neighbour and she was terrified. She was seeing things all the time. She even said that she had seen our mum after she died.'

A final word comes from their step-mother:

It was a traumatic time. These strange incidents often caused problems. For example, just before one Christmas I was in the lounge (it was around that area that things seemed to happen) and I was wrapping the Christmas presents so I said, 'Don't anybody go in'. I went out for a few minutes and left the sellotape in the middle of the floor. I went back in and the sellotape had gone. Of course, I blamed the children. Six weeks later it reappeared exactly where I had left it. That sort of thing caused disagreements in the family.

My cousin had died in that house, so had an elderly lady. I thought it was my turn next, especially after the story of the blue baby. It seemed to me that whatever-it-was seemed to be after the women. So we saved up and bought our own house.

The family left early in the 1970s. They had lived there for 17 years.

EVESHAM

ot many towns have a river on three sides but Evesham is one of them, the town is situated in a loop of the river Avon. Evesham also has a ruined abbey, two beautiful parish churches side by side, a 15th century almonry and a 16th century bell tower.

The Battle of Evesham in 1265 between Simon de Montfort and Prince Edward, later Edward I, is well-known. There is a memorial to him in Abbey Park, a road has been after him, in the museum is a model of the battle and in the grounds of Abbey Manor is an obelisk to the event. Nearly 400 years later, Evesham was again razed to the ground with heavy fighting in the battle between Charles I and the Parliamentarians in the civil war of 1642 to 1646. Yet this seems to have been forgotten. There are no memorials to this event, not even a plaque.

Things had not gone well for the Charles I at Oxford and he had to flee the town, making for Evesham. He could only move slowly as he was hampered by 30 coaches of ladies with their belongings. The king did not feel safe at Evesham, so, on 10th May 1645, he moved on to Pershore.

Colonel Massey, a Parliamentarian, had been defeated at Ledbury and was anxious to make amends, so he decided to capture Evesham as it was one of the gateways to the west. His reinforcements had arrived, so it was a considerable force that assembled outside the town on 25th May, a fortnight after the departure of the king.

Colonel Legge, the Governor, had only a 'scanty force' to withstand the attack. Massey invited him to surrender, but bravely, Legge replied:

You are hereby answered, in the name of His Majesty, that this garrison, which I am entrusted to keep, I will defend so long as I can, with the men, arms and ammunition therein, being nothing terrified at your summons.

As soon as Massey received this reply, he decided to storm the town. On the northeastern side of the town, near Greenhill, were large fortifications with pallisades and a ditch. The bridge from Bengeworth across the Avon on the eastern side of the town was still intact, so was a bridge down the bottom of Boat Lane, where the ferry now runs.

At daybreak, on the 26th May, Massey gave the signal for action. He himself led a party attacking the fortifications. It was extremely dangerous work, they carried huge bundles of twigs and branches to throw into the ditch surrounding the ramparts so that they could get across, and all the time Legge's men were firing down on them. At first the Parliamentarians gave up and fell back, but Massey rallied them and, despite heavy casualties, they reached the ramparts. The conflict lasted over an hour. Then the cavalry managed to break through the defences on the bridges and streamed into the town. Legge rallied his men and fought bravely but his only option was to surrender. Seventy officers and 480 soldiers were taken prisoner.

Massey was hailed as a great hero. On 18th July, a new Parliamentarian governer was appointed for the town.

The loss of Evesham was a serious blow to the king. No longer could he communicate directly with Oxford, Worcester and South Wales. From now on any supplies, arms, or messages going from one place to the other could be intercepted, attacked, and captured.

Royalty at the Royal Oak

Old documents report that Charles II stayed 'in the Royal Oak in Vine Street'. Set in a line of ancient buildings opposite the Market Place, the official age is 15th and 16th century, but parts may be even older. It specialises in Guest Ales and home cooking of traditional pub food, such as steak pies.

In the cellar is a bricked up tunnel which could have reached the nearby river Avon. It opens up all kinds of exciting possibilities. Was it used as a hasty exit for priests in the days of the religious persecutions? More likely, it was used for smuggling contraband from the Avon into the cellars.

The inn has long had the reputation of being haunted. The Royal Oak has eight half-timbered residential rooms and reports of mysterious events have come from room 5.

One of the locals, Rob, used to play golf with the previous owner, Alan, and one busy weekend Alan asked Rob if he could help out as a bartender. That was three-and-a-half years ago and Rob has been there ever since. He says:

The Royal Oak. The king probably stayed here.

Alan always swore the place was haunted. The lights would go on and off – for example you would find the pantry light on when you knew you had switched it off, and the switch was up so the light should have been off. The pictures were often tipped out of alignment, so that he would have to go round in the morning straightening them up. He would straighten them, then the next morning they would be tipped again.

I know that I have had to change a barrel, thinking it was empty because the beer wasn't flowing, I've put a new barrel on and found the old one half full and the floats have been mysteriously pulled in. Often the telephone is ringing but when I go to answer it no-one is there but it seems to happen too often for a call centre to be involved.

Just before Michelle and the new licensee arrived two-and-a-half years ago I was down the cellar one evening , when I felt something press against my left shoulder. The force knocked me back slightly and I felt a large mass push right through me. I went icy cold. Then I heard distinct footsteps and they didn't go up the stairs in front of me, they went across and through a wall. I was petrified.

A grey old lady has been seen in room 5 by several people. One of them was a Dutch lad, he had come over with a party who were working in the greenhouses in Offenham. He said he woke up one night, opened his eyes and there was a grey-haired old woman sitting knitting in the chair by the side of his bed. He closed his eyes and when he opened them again, she had gone. He was really spooked and asked me if I thought he was dreaming. I told him that others have seen the same apparition.

Michelle (the licensee) won't lock up on her own. I have to stay with her until she has gone through the gate, then she leaves me to go out on my own! She won't be left on her own especially at night.

Michelle has been at The Royal Oak for two-and-a-half years. She says that things seem to have quietened down now, but -

For the first six months that we were here, life was horrendous. One day, every toilet was squirting out the top. High up in the lounge bar is a shelf of old bottles and I came down one morning to find every bottle mysteriously placed upside down. I'm certain it wasn't like that when I went to bed.

A friend of mine, Rachel, came in with her 3-year old daughter. The little girl said, 'Stop that man making that noise mummy, I don't like it?'. Her mother asked, 'Which man?' and the little girl pointed to the corner. Nobody was there. She went on, 'Tell the man to stop that banging', Finally she said, 'He's gone now?' Rachel asked, 'Where has he gone' and she replied, 'He's gone along the corridor'.

We had a paranormal society here to carry out tests, my grandchildren came in and said, 'Are they looking for that ghost in the corridor?'.

I would say that the grey old lady in room 5 has been seen six or seven times since I came here.

My living quarters are on the same floor as the guest rooms. I came out of my bedroom one morning and distinctly saw a tall, thin, dark, human-sized shape walk down the corridor. Nearby is a medieval window frame and the white lace curtains were shaking violently. I rushed back into my room and when I came out again the window was open. It's an old window with a secure locking device, no way could that window open by itself and I was the only one on the floor at that time. I was so petrified that I changed the rooms round so that my bedroom is further away from the window.

Over the bar is a sign saying 'Reg and Fred's bar'. The previous licensees told us never to take it down or it will invoke the ghost. I don't think I could cope with another one!

A Wee Experience

A young couple recently moved into a house in the heart of Evesham:

We love Evesham, we have always felt welcome here and all kinds of little things have made us feel at home. For example, we were mourning the death of my father, his name was Andrew and we discovered that we were living right by St Andrew's Church. However, one or two strange things have happened since we moved here, especially in or near our bedroom.

I got up one night to go to the loo and I couldn't see anything but I could sense something. I put the landing light on as quickly as I could and I can

Built over four centuries ago, the Bell Tower is one of the lovely buildings that makes Evesham such a delight.

tell you that it went from a 40 watt to about a 700 watt and went back to 40 watt then died out. I ran into the bathroom, did what I had to do and shot back into bed.

The next day I thought I would investigate the light bulb. Where the light bulb had blown was something that I have never seen before, the prongs had come down and had shot two completely jet black marks on the side of the bulb. The two prongs were pointing down to the floor.

On another occasion I happened to leave the tape recorder running in our bedroom. I played it back the next morning. You could hear something walking on the carpet, a slow swish, swish getting louder as it got nearer, then you heard a scratching and shuffling as if something was picking up the tape recorder and examining it, then came a bump as the tape recorder was put down.

BENGEWORTH

The Story of the Ring

Looking at a map of Evesham, you can see that the town tends to be in two halves. Evesham proper is in the loop of the river but it spreads across the river Avon to the east and southeast and this part is known as Bengeworth. In the twelfth century it was the cause of a bitter dispute between Evesham Abbey and the old Cathedral's monastery at Worcester.

The problem was that both Evesham Abbey and Worcester Monastery stated that they owned the manor of Bengeworth, with all its rights. It was one of the most profitable manors; apart from the house itself there was a fishpool, a number of cottages and a fulling mill. The land was fertile and farmed efficiently. The prior of Evesham Abbey claimed that it was granted to them by the King of the Mercians and/or the king of East Anglia in 708/9, while the Bishop Wulstan of Worcester said that when Cropthorne was given to them by Offa of Mercia in 780, it included Bengeworth. Both the Abbot of Evesham and the Bishop Wulstan were mitred prelates, and no Court of Law dared interfere between two such powerful competitors. The dispute was therefore referred to the court of Bishop Odo in France, who was the brother of William the Conqueror.

For his court evidence, the Abbot of Evesham produced a set of old bones, those of his founder, Saint Egwin. The Bishop Wulstan produced a charter, probably the document for the grant dated 907, authorised by King Alfred who unfortunately died in 901.

The Bishop of Bayeux gave judgement in favour of Bishop Wulstan. An order was sent to the Sheriff of the County, Urse D'Abitot, to take possession of the disputed estates and give them to the Bishop of Worcester.

To show that the command came directly from the Bishop Odo himself and to give the sheriff authority to carry it out, the Bishop sent his signet ring with the decree. In those days the signet ring was used instead of, or as well as, a signature. It was a medieval version of a credit card. The ring had a large face which made an easily identifiable impression when pressed on wax, such as with a wax seal.

The Sheriff took the estates and delivered them to the Bishop of Worcester. That, thought everyone, was the end of that. However, the monks of Evesham Abbey were not happy.

Now, the Sheriff had his castle at Bengeworth at the head of the river. Soon after, he decided to make a pilgrimage to the Holy Land, leaving his castle without proper defences. The monks of Evesham took possession of the castle, burned and demolished it, then consecrated the land. Some old records say that they built the Church of Bengeworth upon the site, others that they merely used it as a cemetery.

Six centuries after the monks had burned down the castle, in 1774, Thomas Beale Cooper was born. He was a kindly man, who always wore a bobbed wig, horn-rimmed spectacles and garters and was five times Mayor of Evesham. It was Beale Cooper who was living in the house now known as the Evesham Hotel, in the 1820s, and planted the huge cedar. Cooper's Lane has been named after him. He inherited that part of Bengeworth which included land next to the church and at the end nearest the church was a curious mound. He decided to level the ground and came across the foundations of a room 42 feet long and 27 feet wide, built of broad limestone with the remains of two fireplaces. The floor was covered with the remains of burned wood and ashes. He guessed that this was the kitchen of the Sheriff's Castle. The document still exists on which he wrote:

'During the careful cleaning of the site, a ring was discovered, bearing the name of Odo. This was probably the signet ring sent by the Bishop of Bayeux to the Sheriff, giving him authority to confiscate the land'.

The Evesham Hotel

In 1539 came the dissolution when Henry VIII closed down all the monasteries, including Evesham Abbey, and took over their property. No doubt the Crown had a great deal of spare land that it was selling off very cheaply, and

Above: Part of the Evesham Hotel.
Below: The rear of the hotel is dwarfed
by the enormous cedar.

about five years later Thomas Watson purchased about 75 acres at Bengeworth including the Manor of Bengeworth and the site of an old Roman camp.

Instead of moving into the Manor House he built a Tudor farmhouse 200 yards away. He named it 'The Mansion House', but it is now known as 'The Evesham Hotel'. There's an old story that the silver bells from Evesham Abbey were hidden in an underground passage between the Mansion House and the Abbey to prevent them being melted down by Henry VIII's men. The original cellar is still there and the fact that the hotel offers 600 different wines indicates its size. Several tunnel-shaped sections of dressed stone have been adjusted or replaced so there could be some truth in the story! In the garden is a ring of six mulberry trees, the originals are said to have been planted by the monks in the 1500s who wanted to breed silkworms but they chose the wrong kind of tree.

The Mansion House must have been quite a large dwelling because Thomas Watson married twice and had 6 sons and 8 daughters. The Watsons were owners for nearly 200 years, after which the house and sixteen acres were sold in 1735 to Benjamin Seward, a London hosier. Seward was a prominent dissenter and John Wesley, founder of Wesleyan Methodism, was a frequent visitor to the house.

In 1972 the owners changed the name to 'The Evesham Hotel' and in 1975 it was bought by the Jenkinson family. The Daily Telegraph has described it as one of the ten best hotels in the British Isles and the Independent, Guardian and Observer have listed it in the top 20.

Like all good old hotels, the Evesham Hotel has, in the past, had its haunted room. The Tudor Room, with its Tudor-type furniture and four-poster bed is the oldest in the house, dating back to about 1540, but the haunting does not occur here, nor in the ancient cellars, but in the lovely attic room at the top of the house. With its sloping ceilings and attic window, it looks like a scene from a Victorian children's book. The present owner, John Jenkinson says:

Until a few years ago, this was a small and rather dingy room, with one attic window and a cupboard of dark wood along the one wall. It gave people an oppressive feeling as soon as they walked into it and perhaps that is why several people, including my own mother-in-law, refused to go in it. The cleaners often remarked that it sent cold shivers up their spines. Several times a guest would come to the Reception Desk and say, 'Could you put me in another room tonight? Room 19 is really spooky'. One gentleman reckoned that he had seen a monk in there, but he admitted he may have been dreaming. We have now refurbished it, we have removed the dark cupboard, redecorated in pale colours and extended it to include an en suite. It's now light and airy and, since refurbishing, we have had no more problems.

Blood on His Hands

If you walk down Bridge Street and across the river into Bengeworth, you can't miss Besty's shop (Besty's Ink Tattoos) on the corner of Port Street. To those who are uninitiated in the art of tattooing, a visit to this shop will convince you that this is art at its aesthetic best, with wonderful swirls and whirls circulating around all manner of creatures. Besty and his wife are both professional tattoo artists. They employ a teenager, Sid, and various staff for the day-to-day tasks. Besty sets the scene:

We have been here for three years, when we first bought the shop it was a right dump. As soon as we moved in we had a strange feeling and it's really spooky at nights. It's always cold in here. We have always thought that something was here but we didn't know what it was and we still don't know.

Besty's wife, Sam, continues:

I lent my 11-year old son the back door key for our house (nothing to do with the studio) and he lost it. Then we all went on holiday and while we were on holiday I bought a new handbag. A couple of months later I had a late appointment at work. My client arrived and I locked the door because I didn't want to be disturbed. When I had finished I closed the shop up and went to get my handbag from the back room. The bag was open , my filofax was on its side in the bag and perched on top of my filofax, balanced on the edge, was my missing back door key.

One evening, seven of us were here and four of us heard horses' hooves outside in the road. We went to have a look but no horses were there.

About two months ago I went to get some clinical waste bags when I heard a young lady laughing behind me. I thought it was a customer so I came out of the back room but nobody was in the shop. I went to my husband who was in the studio working on a gentleman, and I asked if they had been laughing. They looked at me as if I had gone mad. When I came to replace the bags I discovered I had run out. Perhaps whatever-it-was was amused because I had run out of bags and not noticed.

We had been working hard one day so when we had finished we all sat down and had a cup of tea. Then Betsy and I locked up and went home. We came in the next morning, made a cup of tea and it tasted funny. I assumed the milk had gone off and I went out to buy another bottle of milk. The tea still tasted funny. Then Betsy dipped his finger in the sugar and tasted it and it was heavily laced with salt. Nobody had been in, we are the only key-holders and we haven't got any salt in the shop.

Besty and Samantha, professional Tattoo Artists

Besty takes up the story again:

We decided to hold a Holloween night. We set up a night vision camera facing into the studio and sometime between 1.30 and 2 am we picked up and photographed a large white orb the size of a football. We also set the monitor of the TV. When we looked at the footage we saw streams of sparkly lights, like the lights from sparklets, going up and down outside the doorway of my tattoo door. At that time, Sid and I were out in the back room with the door shut and everybody else was in here. Both my friend, Richard, and I saw the shape of a large, thick-set man.

Sam, went out one night and I was here on my own, I had been working late and it was eight or nine o'clock. I cleaned the clips and sterilised the equipment. I was not in a rush to get home. I decided that I was hungry, so I went across the road to get a Chinese, I'm very partial to their curry. I set the table up and was just starting to tuck into my curry when out of the corner of my eye I saw someone walk down and disappear into the studio. I thought, 'Is that a figment of my imagination?'. I carried on eating my dinner and suddenly a huge grey figure emerged on my left hand side from the back room and stood right in front of me, staring at me. He was a big man with a black beard, dark hair and blood on his hands. His apron also had blood on it. I had only just started eating my curry but I threw it at the sink, turned the electricity off, locked up and rushed home. When I told my wife she was in fits of laughter. She didn't think it was so funny when she saw my curry all over the wall the next morning.

Sid has seen him as well, and some of the staff have seen a figure going through that wall where there used to be a doorway going through into next door. That ghost doesn't seem to do a great deal except walk about but I got the impression that he was not nice. He didn't do anything to me but I sometimes feel that he's around and I feel threatened.

A friend of ours, Richard is sensitive to these sort of things and said that he thought it was a butcher who worked next door. When we looked into the history of the place, we discovered that this was once the oldest inn in Evesham, then during the 1800s, next door was divided off and turned into a butcher's shop. We wondered if the salt incident was linked in with the butcher because they used salt to preserve meat, didn't they? We had no idea that it was once a butcher's until we looked into the history.

KIDDERMINSTER

t's surprising that a town as old as Kidderminster should have so few ancient buildings. As far back as 1235 cloth weaving was established here; the river Stour is said to have special properties to enhance colours. As the cloth industry declined, so it was replaced by carpet weaving and, until recent times, it was the great carpet centre of England – in fact, carpets have been exported all over the world, as far away as Australia.

Kidderminster must have been thriving in the 1100s, as Henry II gave the Royal Manor of Kidderminster to Manser Biset. Henry III was nearly murdered here in the 1200s. He was staying in the residential hall of John Biset, which was in the Dudley Street/Orchard Street area, near to St Mary's Church. Margaret, a relative of John's, was also staying there and when she was at her devotions at midnight she heard someone creeping quietly through the building and realised that he was on his way to assassinate the king. She managed to raise the alarm and the intruder was apprehended.

Kidderminster's parish church, too, must have been in existence in 1154 as the Rectory of Kidderminster was given to a convent of 'leprous women' at Maiden Bradley. However, nothing of the present church was built before the fifteenth century. The oldest parts are the massive tower and the sixteenth century aisles and arcades, and these have been heavily Victorianised.

In the church is a monument to Sir Ralph Clare, First Steward of Kidderminster, who was taken prisoner at the Battle of Worcester in 1651. Somewhere in the churchyard is buried a 'poor woman' who had been wounded at the battle of Leicestershire in 1645, together with several soldiers killed in the same year at Trimpley when a Royalist garrison was captured.

Also buried here is Captain Charles Dingham together with one of his soldiers, both were killed in 1646, perhaps in a skirmish at Kidderminster. In that year, the war was coming to an end, the Royalists were on the losing side and matters were desperate. Bravely, a certain Lord Astley gave orders for all men from the different garrisons who would join him, to rendezvous at Bridgnorth. Only 3,000 men arrived; more than half were officers from regiments that had been wiped out. They marched to Kidderminster but a skirmish took place with the Parliamentarians and contemporary reports say that at least 20 were killed.

There were other nasty incidents. Evidently, Worcestershire towns had been sending the required supply of conscripts by using prisoners. They were thus able to get rid of their undesirables, but in the army this was undermining discipline. In fact, it was said that the majority of the soldiers in Royalist garrisons were drunken, dissolute gangs of robbers. The officers decided that this practice must stop. A letter from a Colonel Frazer, dated 6th June1644, states:

'… last night there appeared at Kidderminster at 12 of the clock at night, a party of 120 horse, which threatened the inhabitants to ruin them if they sent any prisoners to your Lordship's army'.

That same year a Royalist force marched through Kidderminster and found it 'little better than an empty farm'.

Especially towards the end of the war, supplies and ammunition were finding it difficult to get through. The army could only exist by plundering. When the Royalists arrived at Kidderminster, one Parliamentarian remarked that they were 'the most rude, ravenous, and ill-governed horse that I believe ever trod upon the earth'.

The vicar of St Mary's at this time was the popular and dynamic Reverend Richard Baxter. As he was featured in 'Ghosts, Murders and Scandals' there is no need to give his biographical details here. A statue of him raises a hand in blessing on the Kidderminster bypass. The creator of popular Christian literature through his book, 'Saints Everlasting Rest', he was at St Mary's, first as curate, then vicar, from about 1641 to 1660. He was a kind and dedicated man who had a great influence on the town.

Reverend Baxter was in bed on the night following the battle when he heard the thundering of hooves from those fleeing from the battle. He later wrote:

Kidderminster being but 11 miles from Worcester the flying army passed, some of them, through the town and some by it. I was newly gone to bed when the noise of flying horse acquainted me with the overthrow, and a few of one of Cromwell's troops that guarded Bewdley Bridge, having tidings of it, came into our street and stood in the open market place, before my door, to surprise them that passed by. And so when many hundreds of the flying army came together, when the 30 troopers cried 'stand' and fired at them, they either hastened away or cried quarter, not knowing in the dark the number it was that charged. And so were as many were taken there as so few men could lay hold on, and till midnight the bullets flying towards my door and windows, and the sorrowful fugitives hastening by for their lives did tell me of the calamitousness of war.

Ghosts at the Kidderminster Shuttle

Blackwell Street existed as a thoroughfare as long ago as the 1700s and probably before that time. Tower Buildings arrived in 1934 and a section is occupied by the Kidderminster Shuttle.

The staff of the Shuttle, who have reported with great enthusiasm on various manifestations over the years, were intrigued to find that their very own building had once housed a ghost. The information comes from a retired typist, who now lives in Clent but worked in the Council's Valuation office for four years. To those of us who are unaware of the work of the Valuation Office, she says that she had a typewriter with a huge carriage and if someone applied to have their rates reduced she had to complete several large forms. She continues:

The manager of the office saw a ghostly female figure several times, mostly in the evenings when he was working late. I think others saw it too, because I was asked if I had seen it. The building has a long corridor that goes from one end to the other, that's where it was seen. We were all warned about it and told not to work late. Then fire doors were fitted and it wasn't seen after that.

The present staff say that, although they haven't actually seen anything, they often feel that someone is behind them, watching them.

Tower Buildings. The Kidderminster Shuttle offices are bottom left.

A few minutes later his colleague suddenly said "That bloke's just walked through that wall". My husband confirmed he had seen the same thing.

Walking Through the Wall

Two police officers had a curious experience in the Horsefair area. One of the wives, Kay, sent us an email:

I thought I would email you a suspected ghost sighting in Kidderminster that my husband related to me. My husband is a police officer and about three years ago he was on duty in Kidderminster along with another male colleague. Both my husband and his colleague are not the sort to be scared by anything easily and I would describe both of them as sceptical of such things as ghosts. It was about 3am, the day and time of year are unknown. Both of them were in a police car in the Horsefair area. They had just travelled from the ring road into the Horsefair heading towards the traffic lights at the junction of Radford Avenue and Broad Street.

My husband then spotted an elderly man walk round the corner out of Radford Avenue towards them. He walked along that side of the road towards the ring road, but after just a few short yards, he walked straight through a wall to his left. My husband thought he was seeing things and didn't mention to his colleague what he had seen for fear of him thinking he was being daft. A few minutes later his colleague suddenly said "That bloke's just walked through that wall". My husband confirmed he had seen the same thing and so they both went to have a closer look. They went to the section of wall that the man had walked through and kicked it a few times to confirm it was solid, and it was.

He describes the man as aged about 60 or 70, with a long grey beard and a long dark coat down to his ankles. He looked solid just like a real person.

We suggested to Kay and her husband that the ghost might be that of Richard Baxter and a further email read:

My husband has looked up Richard Baxter and found a picture of him on this link, (http://members.aol.com/augusteen/Baxter.html) and says that could have been him. He didn't even know who Richard Baxter was as he isn't originally from Kidderminster.

However, Alan Lauder, who runs Kidderminster Ghost Walks (01562 750696 if you want an interesting evening) has other ideas:

This ghost also answers to the description of Ebeneezer Guest, whose apparition has been seen several times in that part of Kidderminster. He lived from 1822 to 1913 and was a rent-collector who tried to clean up the town. The Horsefair was a red light district with many brothels and houses of bad repute.

Oliver Twist at Castle Road

Castle Road is to the south of the town centre, near Brinton Park. It has the unusual distinction of having two waterways passing beneath it, both the Staffordshire & Worcestershire canal and the river Stour. A few years ago, Arthur's son, David, was living there:

David was living in a terraced house in Castle Road, four or five years ago. From the front door you walked into a hall with the front room on your right, then straight into the lounge. Behind the lounge was the kitchen, behind that was the toilet and at the back of the garden was a high brick wall with Kidderminster cemetery behind it.

My son told my wife and I about some strange occurrences that happened in his house whilst he was living there. One evening, when he was in the front room, he saw the image of a little boy. David likened him to one of the urchin-type boys in Oliver Twist. A few days later David had a friend, Paul, staying for the night. During the night Paul had to get up to go to the toilet downstairs at the back of the house. Paul said he happened to look in the direction of the sofa (which was in the lounge) and he saw a little boy lying on the sofa. He rushed upstairs again absolutely terrified. His description of the little boy matched David's. David hadn't said anything to his friend about the previous occurrence.

David asked the next door neighbour if anything unusual ever happened. His neighbour replied, 'Do you mean the little boys?'.

I believe that after David had moved out the new owners were going to somehow convert the inside of the house.

The Crazy Draught

An elderly lady says that when she was living in Welbeck Drive, Blakebrook, there were strange happenings in the house:

My mother used to complain that she could hear me sleepwalking but whenever she went to have a look at me, I was fast asleep in bed.

It was a lovely night, a full moon and no wind. I had just gone to bed when suddenly, my mum's bedroom door slammed shut with a crash that shook the house. There was a great rush of wind through the house and the light in my bedroom went out. The next morning my father said to me, 'How did you manage to unscrew the light bulb out of the holder?' Of course, I hadn't touched it.

The doors and windows had been closed and there was no way a draught could have blown through the house.

The Family Ghost

Stoney Lane is on the northern edge of the town, behind it is the Staffordshire and Worcestershire canal and nearby is an old mill. The area has great potential but has been spoiled by a run-down factory estate.

Paranormal experts suggest that pregnant ladies are particularly suscep-tible to the paranormal, and Mrs Priest was expecting her first baby when she had her first unusual experience:

The first ghost I saw was in 1974 when I was living in Stoney Lane. I was pregnant at the time and had just finished work. We lived in a three storey house and the lounge was on the first floor. All the doors were locked so no-one could wander in.

I was reading and became aware that I was being watched. I looked up and there was a well-dressed man standing across the room from me looking at me. He was not very tall and was dressed in a suit with collar and tie and had a full head of greying hair. I was not afraid, I just thought I was seeing things. I looked down at my book and when I looked up again he had gone.

I related this to my husband on his return from work and he said that I had just described his father. I should add that his father had died at the age of 53 in 1965 before I met my husband and up to that date I had not seen any pictures of him, especially as his mother had remarried.

I gave birth to a daughter in March and she was the first girl to be born in the Priest family for over forty years. My husband always believed that it was his father who had come to see me because he knew I was having a girl and he had had all grandsons.

The second incident was in September of that year. Again it involved my baby daughter. We were going on holiday in the Lake District and had stopped on the way up at the home of my aunt in Blackburn. My mother, myself and my brother's girlfriend were sharing one room with the baby daughter in her carry cot. My brother and husband were in another room and my aunt and her husband slept downstairs. The baby was very fractious and I could not get her to settle at all. I had got out of bed on several occasions to try to settle her to no avail. I began to get out of bed yet again when I became aware of a woman standing at the bottom of the bed. She appeared to be the same age as my mother with similar hair. The room was lit by the street light. I was unsure that it was my mother but stayed in bed, and the baby went quiet. This woman then seemed to drift out of the room. I then realised it was not my mother and to be really honest I was afraid to

*Near Stoney
Lane*

get out of bed to check on my daughter and waited until morning. The baby was fine. The next morning I went downstairs and asked my mother if she had got out in the night. She said that she hadn't, she had been sleeping with her back to the room and thought that I had tried to settle the child. I then asked my aunt if she had come up into the bedroom because the baby was crying and again she said that she hadn't. I was beginning to think I had imagined the whole thing when my brother's girlfriend came in and asked if I was talking about the woman at the foot of the bed during the night! Obviously I was not imagining it.

My aunt asked around the neighbourhood but could find nothing out.

Glowing Hands

Although the next story is only a few lines, it's one of the most terrifying in the book. It was told by a young lady who lives in Kidderminster:

I woke up in the middle of the night. It was pitch dark but to my surprise, I saw a movement in the corner of the bedroom. Then I saw that there was something coming out of the wall. Two glowing hands appeared out of the corner, they were young, female hands. I screamed but no noise came out of my mouth. I switched the light on quickly and it had all disappeared. I know that I wasn't asleep.

THE MALVERNS

 trange fancies befell me, and fairy-like dreams,
I was weary of wand'ring, and went to repose
On a broad green bank, by a burn-side;
As I lay there and leaned and looked on the waters,
I slumbered and slept, they sounded so merry.
Came moving before me a marvellous vision.

This enchanting poem comes from 'The Vision concerning Piers the Plowman', written 700 years ago in the 1300s by William Langland. He was born in 1332 at a farm in Ledbury and for many years was in minor orders at Little Malvern Priory. His poetry is particularly interesting because of the way in which it describes the life of ordinary folk in the 1300s.

William Langland is just one of the many writers, artists and poets who have been inspired by the grandeur and beauty of the Malvern Hills, among them Byron, Southey, Bernard Shaw, Francis Brett Young and above all, Sir Edward Elgar, whose remains now lie in a churchyard at Little Malvern. A lesser known celebrity is Dr Peter Mark Roget who wrote the indispensable Roget's Thesaurus.

Malvern is not one town, but six. The chief residential centre is Malvern Wells. Great Malvern lies on the eastern slopes of the hills, Malvern Link is on the plain below, and North Malvern is the extension of Great Malvern. West Malvern faces the mountains of Wales while Little Malvern clusters round its priory.

From the top of the Malvern Hill the sites of six battlefields can be seen, Evesham, Mortimer's Cross, Tewkesbury, Worcester, Edgehill and Shrewsbury, while, on the Herefordshire Beacon, are the remains of the British Camp, thought to be the site of a great battle against the Romans.

During the Civil War the Malverns apparently saw only skirmishes. For example, a party of Parliamentarians from Herefordshire crossed the hill and came upon a body of some 50 Royalists. Completely surprised, they were not able to offer any great resistance, and 50 horses and 28 prisoners were taken.

It was Madresfield Court, four miles away, that saw the action. The owner, Colonel Lygon, was a Parliamentarian. By the end of 1646 his troops had been turned out and it was garrisoned for the king. The house was well-stocked with provisions and ammunition and was reckoned to be able to hold out against a siege for three months. However, the Parliamentarians promised the Captain of the garrison that if he gave up the house, he would be paid £200, his troops would each receive 30 shillings (£1.50) and his foot soldiers ten shillings (50p), providing they left all their ammunition and provisions behind. The terms were accepted.

Malvern's Martyr Saint

In about 1016 the Danes attacked a little cell at Deerhurst, and one of the monks, Saint Werstan, fled twelve miles north to live in the Malvern Hills. He was apparently murdered and a man known as 'Guido' was implicated. Saint Werstan's work was continued by Aldwyn, who established Malvern Priory. Malvern began as a settlement outside the priory, probably in about 1085.

The beautiful Priory church with its exquisite windows and misericords is now part of Great Malvern. Until the sixteenth century, the townsfolk had a miserable little church standing in the corner of the present churchyard, and they looked upon the Priory Church with great envy. When Henry VIII dissolved the monasteries, local people bought the great Priory Church and saved it for posterity.

It's no use a town having an interesting history if no-one knows about it, and fortunately Malvern has two lively professional historians who have published a whole series of books about the area. The latest book by Cora Weaver and Bruce Osborne has been published in conjunction with Friends of Malvern Springs and Wells and covers the life of Malvern's tragic martyr. Cora writes:

> There is a long tradition in Malvern of a ghost monk being seen in the vicinity of the top of the 99 steps up to St Ann's well. This was the general location of St Werstan's hermitage and the monk is believed to be him. He is the patron saint of Malvern Springs and Wells and now the subject of extensive scholarly work. There have been many inaccurate and misleading conclusions drawn about this early Malvern martyr and only now is a credible picture emerging of his life and the contribution he made as the founder of the religious establishment in Malvern. The main sources of evidence concerning his life are the medieval Founders Windows in Malvern Priory, however early documentary sources are also being reappraised.

> The hermit Werstan initially lived in a cave, later building a small chapel. His martyrdom occurred in the early 1050s when the Celts attacked the area. Werstan's hermitage, near the present day St Ann's Well, became the founding site for the first formal religious centre during the reign of Edward the Confessor. This led to the eventual establishment of the Priory and Malvern town itself. It is likely that the spring was venerated in the early days as a healing spring named St Werstan's Well, after the martyred saint. This gave rise to the long-standing tradition of it being a healing and spa well. After his premature death, Werstan was replaced by Aldwyn and

The Martyrdom of St Werstan - from Malvern Priory window.

the Benedictine monastery started to grow. The naming of the well as St Ann's occurred much later and was probably a contraction in time of the original name or just an error.

Further information on St Werstan can be found in 'The Illumination of St Werstan the Martyr' by Cora Weaver and Bruce Osborne, available from Cora at 4 Hall Green, Malvern, Worcs, WR14 3QX, or send your details by email to Cora at cora@malvernspa.com, or for details see www.malvernspa.com. Price £9.99 includes P&P.

The Intruder

A Malvern resident tells us:

At Great Malvern Priory, the custodian (then a chap called Charlie Smith) saw something one evening in the priory. He was just locking up for the night and was standing at the main door on the north side, when he saw a figure walking past the glazed inner door - someone still in the priory. Thinking he was locking a visitor in he called out "I'm locking up!" and opened the door again for whoever it was to come out. Although Charlie searched the priory he found nobody.

The Shadow of Raggedstone Hill

There were once two Priories in Malvern, one at Great Malvern as described above and a smaller Benedictine Priory in Little Malvern, founded in 1171 at the foot of the Herefordshire Beacon. The Little Malvern Priory Church has been partly rebuilt and now exists as St Giles' Church. Associated with the Little Malvern Priory is a tragic tale about a monk.

Towards the end of the 1800s the local vicar, Reverend Symonds, claimed to have seen a bundle of papers in the attic of a friend, telling the story of the Shadow of Raggedstone Hill. The story was rewritten by Charles Grinrod, a popular Victorian author and became a best-seller. According to the story, in the 1400s a monk from Little Malvern Priory fell foul of priory rules. He married a distant relative to save her from marrying an unwanted suitor, and he was caught up in a family feud and committed murder. As a punishment, the Prior ordered him to climb up Raggedstone Hill every day on his hands and knees. He became weaker and weaker until, a year later, when he reached the top of the hill, he died. With his last breath he cursed the hill, saying:

> My curse be on thee, thou heaven blasting hill, and on those which laid this burden upon me and all that be like as they are … May thy shadow and my shadow never cease to fall upon them.

Among the victims of the shadow are thought to be the Prior of Malvern, who died soon afterwards and two frequent visitors to the Priory - Sir John Oldcastle, a priest who was burned at Smithfield and Cardinal Wolsey, who failed to persuade the Pope to annul Henry VIIIs marriage to Catherine of Aragon.

Further information comes from a retired housewife:

> The shadow of Raggedstone Hill was said to fall on Castlemorton Church. All kinds of strange things happened there. My grandfather, George Hammond, was the Church Warden in the early 1900s and he told me lots of stories but unfortunately, I

Left: Castlemorton Church in Victorian times. Right: North Hill, Malverns.

can only remember the following.

In those times, the Church Warden was often the local gravedigger, and this was so in my grandfather's case. There was an elderly couple living in Castlemorton parish, unfortunately the husband died and my grandfather buried him in the churchyard. About a year later, his wife also died and she should have been buried next to her husband. However, both the coffin and the body of her husband had completely disappeared. The gravediggers have a map showing where people are buried and he dug all round the area but couldn't find the coffin. He dug right down, much deeper than he usually went, but it wasn't there. Over the years he dug many other graves in different parts of the churchyard but the coffin and the body of the husband was never found.

The Malvern Beast

From the wilds of Worcestershire come tales of phantom animals, together with accounts from those who are certain that they have seen something that looks as if it has escaped from a zoo. Does anyone have an explanation for the animal seen by Oliver Webb's father?

My Dad took up walking a few years ago. He began by walking a lot locally, but culminated in crossing Dartmoor north to south in a

day (an epic walk he'd been working towards for ages) just two years ago. His practice walks began at his home at Storridge and went up Whitman's Hill, along to the west side of North Hill, then up onto the ridge of the Malvern hills and the full distance to Chase End Hill at the southern tip. Then back again. He did this many times. On one occasion he came face to face with a huge black cat - not a domestic cat, but something the size of an Alsatian dog, though most definitely a cat - it had a long low curving tail like a leopard or something. It came out of the bracken and undergrowth to one side of the path, took a hard look at Dad and then slipped into the undergrowth again and was gone. Dad said he was pretty shaken by it, although it only lasted a few seconds. He told Mum and me about it, but didn't mention it to anyone else in case people thought he was being a bit daft. This happened about three years ago. Since then, completely out of the blue, we've met two other people who have had nearly identical experiences in the same area. We came to meet them because my Dad contracted cancer and both the other men were in the same situation.

Screams from a Baby

A few years ago a young couple moved into Pickersleigh Road:

We lived in Malvern when our youngest child was born until she was one year old, and found it to be a beautiful but very eerie place indeed. We discovered how quiet it could be, almost deathly quiet at night, and considering it is rural, not many birds would be around. A cemetery was located not far from us, which, when we cut through it at night just as it was getting dark, was atmospheric with the Malverns as a backdrop.

The first thing we noticed in our house off the Pickersleigh Road was that it always had electrical problems: bulbs would go constantly, lights would dim regularly and sometimes in answer to our questions! The baby would constantly watch the ceiling light as if someone was talking to her from there - when we changed her nappy - looking puzzled, we could see her eyes examining whatever it was in great detail. As she got a little older, say 8 months old, she would become so terrified when in her cot at night that she would literally scream as if frightened by someone, and then throw herself out of the cot onto the floor - she couldn't even walk then, so she must have been terrified.

I remember reading about Malvern's history as a chanting centre for pilgrims in days gone by, and that there is a curse placed upon it by a monk, so maybe that explains why it felt so strange.

It Wasn't Possums

Here is another story from the residential part of the town, again by a young person:

I lived in a flat in Albert Park Road, Great Malvern. The house was over 100 years old. The owners were just starting to do it up and had finished the flat at the top of the house. It had obviously been the servants' quarters, the little old fireplaces were still there. I got into it through a door at the back of the house. There was a kitchen on your right and what was obviously the servants' quarters on your left. Then I went up a tiny staircase, as the servants had done.

I moved in and kept hearing strange noises. I assumed they were coming from other parts of the house. I had just come back from Australia and there I would have thought it had been possums, but here I supposed it was squirrels or something. The bedroom was cold and smelt funny. The windows kept opening by themselves. If you could see them you would know how difficult that was, they were wooden and warped. I would be in one room and the window would bang in another room. Then I would be in that room and the window would bang somewhere else. I started to get frustrated. I thought, there's something wrong with the house. I thought it was a through draft or something similar.

There was so much noise one night I spoke to the owners downstairs. I said, 'Something is going on in the attic'. They said, 'Oh no, there's

Remains of Little Malvern Priory. A monk from this priory placed a curse on those upon whom the shadow of Raggestone Hill should fall.

nothing up there. Anyway we will go and have a look', but it was quite clear. The noises didn't seem to stop.

I said to the owner of the house, 'If I didn't know better I would think I had a little visitor who would like to live where I'm living in the house'. I wasn't too bothered, but she freaked out. She went straight out and organised two people to come. They were more annoying than anything. I said, 'I'm not having any part of this'. I went out but when I came back, the flat smelt differently, especially in the one bedroom. I put that down to the ladies' perfume. I also thought it felt different, it was warmer.

The next morning I spoke to the owner. She told me that the ladies said there was an old gentleman who wouldn't leave the bedroom I was in. In the end they found his son who came and took him away.

I thought, 'That's weird. I'm not buying into this. I don't want to know'. But the noises stopped and it felt different.

The Flight

Elizabeth now lives in Malvern but she trained as a nurse in Cumbria.

I was working up in Cumbria in 1992, I had just qualified and I was working as a nurse in a nursing home. There was myself and two other carers, we were doing night duty. I was booked for two night shifts and that was the first. It was a very old building, I think it was Edwardian. It had got a number of floors, the main staircase was very grand and was overlooked by a stained glass window. The home was in two parts, ours was for the elderly frail but not mentally impaired.

We were sitting downstairs when we heard footsteps above us. We went upstairs to see which resident was out of bed and walking round but everybody was in bed. There was only one flight of stairs to that particular part of the house so no-one could have left the bedrooms. As soon as we sat down we heard the footsteps again. Again we went upstairs and again no-one was out of bed. This happened three times. Every time, as soon as we sat down we would hear the footsteps upstairs. Every time we went up everybody was still in bed. We gave up in the end and ignored the footsteps.

A carer came across to speak to us from the other half of the home. She walked in and said, 'Oh, the evil one is out tonight!'. We hadn't told her anything about what had been going on. We hadn't told her we had heard footsteps.

After she had gone we heard it again. We had to go upstairs then in case someone had got out of bed. There was one elderly lady who was awake. She was looking at something in the corner of her room and screaming 'Get out! Get out!'.

In the morning we handed over to the day staff and told them about it. They said they knew which room it was. They told us that many years ago, a train track ran close to the house. The train had crashed into the house and killed a baby sleeping in there, which was thought to be that room.

When we went to investigate the footsteps we used the huge staircase in the front hall but in the morning, when we did the laundry, we used a back staircase. I just got the willies and came down so quickly that I twisted my ankle. I phoned in sick and never went back. I resigned.

THE SUCKLEY HILLS

To the north, the Malverns peter out in a series of gentle undulations, known as the 'Suckley Hills'. This is a magical part of Worcestershire, immortalized by the Victorian Antiquarian, Jabez Allies, who documented tales of strange animals, phantom coaches and horses, screaming apparitions and a variety of unusual sightings in that area.

On the western side is Suckley village. In the 1200s it was owned by the infamous King John, whose effigy in Worcester Cathedral is well-known. He gave it to the Prince of North Wales, Llewelyn ap Jorweth, when his daughter, Joan, married the Prince. Llewellyn also used the manor of Suckley as dowry when his daughter married the Earl of Chester. However, the English and the Welsh came to blows so the King took his gift back again! Henry III later restored it to the Earl.

Happily Haunted

Stonemason Oliver Webb, meets many people through his work and has very kindly collected up their paranormal experiences for us, for instance, he gave us the Worcester Cathedral story in the first chapter. He became interested in the paranormal after some strange events in his life:

Over the years a good few incidents have happened to our family - none of which have been exactly earth shattering.

I was brought up in Suckley in a pair of old black and white cottages (though I believe it was once three) and my grandparents lived next door. Both families moved there in 1961 - just before I was born - and remained there until 1984, when my grandfather died. In the early days of our tenure the two houses were separate with no interconnecting access, though this was changed in the 1970s.

During our time there, a lot of odd little instances happened. The first incident that I have heard of happened at Christmas 1962 when I was a baby of 8 months old. The house was so cold that my parents put me to bed in my pram downstairs in the living room (where the only source of heat was). Dad, apparently, tucked me in last thing at night and switched all the lights off. In the morning he was also the first to rise and was surprised to find that the Christmas tree lights (new that year, and still in use today) had plugged themselves in and switched themselves on during the night. I was not yet walking and certainly too little to escape from my pram. Mum and Dad were always most particular about unplugging everything at night, there were only two electrical sockets in the room.

A telephone in my grandfather's hallway always gave a little 'ting' when the receiver was replaced, it continued to do so occasionally even after it was disconnected. Grandfather's study door was heard to slam shut when the house was empty (actually when it was being cleared and I was there on my own) and a cat named Chloe who had a most distinctive call was heard by all of our family members independently both inside and outside the house for some months after she had died on the road.

In the early 1970s we converted half of a room at the back of the house (once used as a milking parlour, possibly, since it had a black brick floor with a gutter running the length of the house) into a bathroom. The finished bathroom was quite small and had no opening window - only a fixed skylight. On more than one occasion my father went into the bathroom early in the morning to find the light switch pull cord swinging wildly to and fro. We tried everything we could think of to make it happen, but never managed to discover the reason. The bathroom door was always left ajar and one approached it through what amounted to a junk room, which also had no opening window, and the light's pull cord was visible before one entered the bathroom.

On several occasions over a period of some ten years my Dad, who worked on night shift and returned home at around 3.00am, walked into the kitchen upon arriving home to find the egg timer running (an old fashioned hour glass with sand in it).

One night when I was about 15, I woke up in the early hours, aware that something was happening in my room. I slept with the door closed and the light off, so the room was inky black, though it had three little windows (two west facing, one south). The windows had thin curtains, but the outline of the windows was just visible through them. Between the two west facing windows, at about waist height, there came an irregular flashing light. It was a white light, quite bright and about the size of an A4 sheet of paper. It flashed on and off - each "on" lasting maybe a second - sometimes slightly longer, sometimes quicker - and the "offs" lasting several seconds at a time. I endured it for maybe ten minutes, initially surprised, then very scared, before making a dash for the door and the light switch. I can be absolutely definite that I was awake - this wasn't a half-asleep semi-dream, after about twenty or so of these flashes I was not just awake but charged with adrenaline! There was no traffic along the lane, and no street lights, or lights from other houses, etc. The only electrical items in the room were a ceiling light and an Anglepoise desk light.

The house was, by 1984, needing a large amount of money spent on it and my parents were unable to afford to stay. The old cottage was a lovely home and is full of happy memories

The Phantom Burglar

If you intend to rig up a burglar alarm, remember this young man's story and don't do it in the Suckley Hills!

One of our neighbours at the top of Birchwood Lane had suspected that someone had been prowling around their garden at night, so Dad

The Suckley Hills

be thief (Dad had been very active as an amateur astronomer in the
1960s and early 1970s). So Dad and I set up a long string across the
path leading from the driveway and a load of old oil cans and tins
tied to one end – these were then stood on a wall in such a way that if
someone walked through the string the cans would all fall down with
a crash.

In the early hours that night the whole lot went off with a tremendous
crash and we duly rushed out into the garden but found nobody. We
suspected an animal might have triggered it so the following evening
we modified the set up – raising the string to chest height. It went off
that night, too. We suspected the string might be shrinking in the dew
so more slack was allowed – it went off that night. We tried everything
– placing the cans more securely, changing the location slightly,
different string (also cotton and thin wire), different heights, different
ironware, but it went off every single night without fail. After a week
or more we got so sick of it that we abandoned the idea!

Nobody ever apparently prowled around, but something set
off Dad's alarm every single night – definitely not the actions of a
burglar, of that we had become quite certain! We had no immediate
neighbours, the house below was empty and the next one beyond that
was Mosewick Farm at Longley Green, above us was an old lady, a
couple with two tiny children and another single elderly woman – our
house was quite isolated.

PERSHORE

here are just a few towns that seem to get more attractive and interesting as time goes by and Pershore is one of them. Clustered round the old Norman Abbey, the streets have a range of shops and small stores – including three bookshops. One of them, Arcade bookshop, has the remains of an old chapel in the basement and Mrs Payne, the owner, says that she can tell whether the ghost likes you or not as to whether the atmosphere goes warm or cold as you go down the stairs!

During the time of Civil War and the events of 1651, great armies tramped through the Midlands. They often settled in and around various towns, and orders went out to local suppliers for vast quantities of food and beer. Sometimes they were paid, sometimes not. The night before the Battle of Worcester, about 28,000 Parliamentary troops were stationed in and around Pershore.

However, this is reckoned to be only half the number of Royalists that passed through it during the earlier Civil War. In 1644 Charles I was in a desperate position. Two Parliamentary armies were closing in on him, planning to trap him in Oxford, so he and his army escaped quietly at dead of night, slipping between two enemy armies. Some historians reckon that his army numbered 60,000 with 30 coaches of women and 30 of supplies. The Parliamentarians could not believe it when they awoke in the morning and found that he was missing, and they set off in hot pursuit.

As he hurried along, he ordered that bridges should be destroyed behind him to delay the Parliamentary army. He stayed temporarily in Evesham but did not feel safe there so he went on to Pershore. The bridge here was blown up in such a hurry that all the troops failed to get safely over. Two or three officers, their Major and 26 privates were drowned as well as some 80 countrymen, whose hats were picked up floating down the river. Charles pushed on to Worcester and lodged in the Bishop's Palace.

The High Street Coach and Horses

Janet Daniels and Marion Freeman have written a series of small books about Pershore. They found that they had a whole series of quirky little items that they thought would make interesting reading but didn't fit into any theme, so they produced *Pershore Digest,* and in it is the following information:

We were manning a stall at a Family History Fair when we were approached by a lady who had worked as a dental nurse for Maurice Banbury at Lincoln House in Pershore High Street. At that time, around 1975, they used to hold a late surgery on a Tuesday evening.

On one such evening, as they were cleaning up, this lady heard the noise of horses and what sounded like a cart coming up the High Street towards Worcester. She mentioned this to Mr Banbury, the dental surgeon, who told her to look out of the window, which she did but could see nothing. He later told her that he had, on more than one occasion, seen the front part of a coach and a coachman with a whip leading horses, the coach leaving the archway of the Angel Inn and travelling towards Worcester.

As we were chatting, another lady joined us saying she too had heard the sound of horses at the same spot, but again had seen nothing. In her case, she had been in the same area on the opposite side if the street, being on an errand for her mother. Further conversation revealed that both events had occurred during the 1970s and had taken place in the evening dusk at around the same time of night.

Janet and Marion suggest that this might be an old Pershore coachman by the name of John Goore. But could it not be something connected with the Civil war – perhaps a straggler from the 30 coaches of women? There would be more tension and terror in the latter suggestion, and more likely to leave an impression on time.

The Highwayman and the Angel

The Pershore Digest also has two pages of information on the well-known highwayman, Captain Thomas Dangerfield. Born in 1650, he was imprisoned many times for theft and counterfeiting. At one time he was involved in a Catholic plot against Charles II. He was arrested on a charge of felony but escaped from prison to roam the Worcestershire countryside as a highwayman. He was re-arrested and on his way from Newgate to Tyburn had an argument with a barrister who hit him with his cane. The cane entered Dangerfield's eye and he died two hours later from the injury. The barrister was brought to trial and executed for the highwayman's murder!

Despite this eventful life, Dangerfield managed to keep a diary and in it he wrote:

"Wed. December 17 ... came to Easam (Evesham) and there not being pleased by the man at the Crown, I went to the Angell at Parshore where I lay all night'. The following day he called at the Angel again but only stayed for dinner, which cost him five shillings.

The Angel was an important coaching inn for the wealthy. It was also a posting house, where the mail coaches would change horses, and collect and deliver any mail. The mail was then taken out to the surrounding district by 'postboys' – the postboys could be any age. Evidently, they slept overnight at The Angel because the proprietor in 1932 remembers seeing their beds in the stables. He said they looked like a row of coffins filled with straw.

Such an old hostelry often has a ghost or two and the owner/manager, Juan Mendez, has no doubt that the hotel is haunted. He has heard footsteps overhead when no-one is there. Fortunately, the ghost only puts in an appearance in the dining room, so that visitors can be assured that they sleep undisturbed. Mr Mendez says that all those who have seen him describe him as a large man, well-dressed. The best description comes from Gerald Wigley and was first published in 'Haunted Pubs and Hotels' (Hunt End Books, 1998). Unfortunately, Gerald has now passed away but his wife said:

We often stayed at the Angel Inn at Pershore and in 1994, we decided to spend our Easter holiday there. The dining room was quite full on the Friday evening. We sat in the bay on the left hand side and I was facing Gerald with my back to the fireplace. Suddenly, he looked up and saw the figure of a man standing in front of the fireplace. His first thought was that it was Mr Mendez and he said to himself, 'That's

The Angel Inn and Posting House, once popular with a highwayman!

a funny place to stand'. It was between two tables which were quite close and there wasn't really room for anyone to stand there. Three ladies were at the one table and I forget who was at the other. When he told me I turned round to look but couldn't see anything. I said, 'Where is it?' but evidently it had faded away.

Then it reappeared. My husband said, with his hand over his mouth, 'There it is again, look!' but I didn't like to keep turning round. People would start staring. Apparently it faded away and reappeared yet again. He saw it three times quite clearly in about two minutes.

I asked Gerald to describe it. My husband was an ex-naval man and he said that the figure was wearing an old naval square rig uniform, a dark blue donkey jacket with buttons. When I pressed for more details, he added, 'You know, you've seen it in old war films'. I also asked him about the hat but I can't remember what he said.

He didn't seem at all surprised. I asked him how he felt now that he had seen a ghost and he said, 'I feel privileged'.

We told Mr Mendez and he said that the ghost had been seen before in the same spot.

A satisfactory conclusion to this story would have been to suggest that the ghost was that of Thomas Dangerfield but unfortunately the highwayman was quite different in appearance with a 17th century buttoned up coat and a short periwig.

Mr Mendez says that the last strange happening in the hotel was about two years ago:

It was about one o'clock in the morning, the bar was closed and everything was quiet. I was sitting with my wife and about eight of the staff in the lounge and we were having a bite to eat. We were talking about ghosts and suddenly, one of the plates on the wall shattered. It absolutely exploded! We didn't finish our meal, we left it there and ran away!

A Final Note

If you do visit Pershore, don't forget to call in at the town loo, set in the Abbey walls. This is probably the nearest you will get to an out-of-this-world experience in Pershore. Heavenly music greets you as you open the door, there is a ghostly flush and a disembodied voice gives instructions. Providing the system is working, if you open the door without washing your hands a reproachful voice follows you out, 'You have not washed your hands!'.

REDDITCH

o other town has such a wealth of greenery as Redditch. Even the main roads are lined with hedges and trees which are particularly beautiful in the autumn, when they glow with a variety of colours. A huge park, the Arrow Valley Park, runs through the town from north to south. Redditch was designated a new town in 1963, and the Redditch Development Corporation were given miles of farmland on which to build a town. They were determined to preserve as many hedges and trees as possible and create a town where every occupant should have easy access to open countryside. In this they have been largely successful.

However, Redditch history goes right back to about 1140 when a dozen white-robed monks arrived from Garenden Abbey in Leicestershire to found a large Cistercian monastery. It became very prosperous through the wool trade and was at one time the fifth wealthiest Cistercian monastery in England and Wales. The meadows on which it stood have been preserved, largely through the good work of the Bordesley Historical Society. They are, so archaeologists say, one of the most interesting sites in Europe as nothing has been built on them since the monastery closed.

By the time that the civil war broke out in 1642, Henry VIII had closed the monastery and Redditch was simply a little farming community, although nearby villages such as Beoley and Grafton suffered badly. These are included in the 'Villages' section.

During the 1600s, no-one knows quite when and how, Redditch folk acquired such an expertise in needle-making that they were later joined by needlemakers from London, Buckinghamshire, Scotland, Wales and all across England to become the centre of needle-making and its offshoots, fish-hooks and springs. Some needles, springs and fish-hooks are still made here.

Strange Goings-On at Forge Mill

On the edge of the Bordesley Abbey Meadows, down Needle Mill Lane, are two adjacent museums. The first is the Visitor's Centre, which deals with the history of Bordesley Abbey. Next to it is the seventeenth century Forge Mill, probably the only water-powered needle scouring mill still in existence in the world. It was still working in 1958, then it fell into ruin and was rescued by a team of dedicated volunteers. Finally it was saved by the Redditch Development Corporation and opened as a museum by the Queen in 1983. The whole history of needle-making is preserved here. Perhaps the most interesting part is that preserving the old scouring beds. The needles were

77

When he got upstairs, he was astonished to find no-one was there. It was only when he came down that we remembered that we had locked the doors behind us. We both heard those female voices.

coated with various pastes, wrapped tightly into bundles and put under huge flat blocks that moved to and fro, polishing and scouring the needles. The factory is dark, the windows are small and everything looks more or less just as it was left when the mill closed down, with worn pans and tins, oil-covered tools and grimy floor. There is no better environment to evoke the ghosts of the past:

Volunteers say that when they accompany staff taking schoolchildren down the stairs to the scouring mill floor, one or two of the children often draw back in fear. Several times, a volunteer has thought that someone was in the scouring mill and has been talking to the person, only to discover that no-one is there. One of the guides was so certain that she saw a figure that she called out 'Excuse me, we're closing now' but the place was empty. A Ghost Club held a paranormal investigation one night and managed to record a noise that sounded as if it could have been women's and children's voices.

Rachael, Education Officer, has been involved with the mill since 2004:

You do hear creaks and noises because the whole place is really old and creepy but you get used to the noises over the years so that you know which noises are normal and which are not. I was working late one afternoon in the office, everyone else had gone home. The place was all locked up, even the outer door of the office, and I knew that no-one could get in. Without any doubt I heard footsteps walk through the gallery and come towards the locked office door. I waited in fear and trembling for whatever-it-was to come through the door but nothing happened. This wasn't the first time I have heard someone walking about when the place is closed. They're always a woman's footsteps. Other staff stamp about upstairs sometimes and you can hear clomp, clomp, clomp. These mysterious footsteps are quick and light.

Another time I was working in the office - it must have been during last December because the museum was closed to the public - Jo-Ann (my colleague) was here but it was one of those days when I didn't know where she was, she had a lot of work to do across the site. I was working in my office but I had some photocopying to do so I went upstairs and through the gallery to do the photocopying. I heard the front entrance door go. The front door is really heavy, you have to push it open and it gives a loud groan. Then I heard footsteps cross the floor. I thought, 'That must be Jo-Ann coming back'. I stopped photocopying and called ' Jo, I'm upstairs!' There was no reply. I thought, 'She hasn't heard me'. I shouted again, louder. I came downstairs and no-one was about. I thought, 'She must be looking for me'. It was only then that I remembered I had locked the main museum door so that no-one could get in. I absolutely freaked out. I locked up and went home.

However, I must say that although we often feel that someone else is here, we never actually feel threatened.

The Keeper of Collections, Jo-Ann, is the official key holder.

I had an alarm call-out at 4 o'clock early one morning; it came from the scouring mill. My husband, Richard, came with me. When we have a call-out, we follow a certain routine, first we put the lights on, then we lock the doors behind us. We walked into the scouring mill and stood in the main part, on the mill floor. We were both dead tired. Then we heard two female voices upstairs. We looked at each other in surprise. In a case like that, you forget that you have locked the doors and Richard thought somebody had followed us in. He ran all the way upstairs shouting, 'You shouldn't be here, the mill's closed!'. When he got upstairs, he was astonished to find no-one was there. It was only when he came down that we remembered that we had locked the doors behind us. We both heard those female voices.

The footsteps and the voices seem to be female, which would tie in with the fact that the upper floor was used for fly dressing. A huge variety of coloured feathers, scraps of silk and other bits and pieces were tied on to the fish hooks to imitate the movement of insects to tempt the fish to have a nibble. The work required nimble fingers and so it was always done by women.

There's an old story that one of the workers had an affair with the man who owned the mill. Eventually he grew bored with her and rejected her. She was distraught; she had thought that he really loved her, and, too late, she realised that she was nothing to him. She threw herself from a window into the pound at the back of the mill, where she drowned. Her body was swept into the mill wheel, where it jammed the wheel. Her body was torn to pieces. The workers have never recovered all of her and that's why she comes back, looking for the missing parts of her body.

A Pair of Eyes

The next story comes from Forge Mill Road which is, of course, adjacent to the Museum:

We have been in this house for 32 years. My son is now in his forties but when he was about 19 he had been to his girl friend's and they were going out, but he had forgotten his money. So he rushed back into this house without putting the lights on and ran upstairs. In the corner of his bedroom was a chair and sitting in it was a dark figure. A light picked up a pair of eyes. The light went across the eyes and he could see that there was form in the chair.

When he told me about it the next morning I told him, 'Don't be silly', and he said, 'I'm telling you, somebody was there'. So that was that.

There was an aunty who was very fond of him and she hadn't been to see him before she died. She passed away in Smallwood Hospital at nine o'clock, and that was just about the same time that my son went into his bedroom to collect his money. We said, 'That's Aunty come to say 'goodbye'.'

Twenty-odd years later, in the September, his son, who is now 19, come to stay with me – over the years he has stayed with me a lot. I had gone to bed and he was downstairs watching the tv. He happened to look over to the corner of the room and he saw a dark figure. He told us about it the next morning. It really upset him.

The family who lived here before us were a tragic family and we wondered if that was anything to do with it.

Others might point out that the house is on the edge of the Bordesley Abbey Meadows and many a dark monk has been seen wandering around Redditch. An intriguing fact is that Bordesley was a Cistercian Abbey where the monks wore white. However much of the work, such as looking after farms and the manual labour, was done by Lay Brothers who wore a brown habit. They were under vows of celibacy and obedience but were exempt from the studies and religious services required of the monks. Models of monks and lay-brothers can be seen in the museum.

A Sporting Apparition

As the needle industry developed, the population grew from a tiny village to 1,000 in 1800, 13,500 in 1900, and 32,000 in 1963. As the town multiplied, so did the public houses. In his book, 'Old Redditch Pubs' Alan Foxall quotes from the Temperance League of 1894:

'Redditch is notably a drunken, immoral town. … There are 84 public houses in our midst and we spend £42,000 per annum on intoxicating drink. That gives an average income of £500 to each licence holder.'

In those days £2 a week was a good wage! There were so many pubs at Headless Cross that the nail-makers of Bromsgrove walked the seven miles from Bromsgrove to drink there.

In 1830 the legislation regarding alcohol was changed, and anyone could sell beer for the cost of a £2 licence providing they were of good character. Many drinking establishments opened about this period and the Sportsmans Arms, in Redditch, seems to be one of them. It was licensed in 1854 to Thomas Rikards, who was also a dairy farmer. Towards the end of the 1900s, Paul Dyson was the licensee:

The first I heard of the ghost was during the 1960s when some friends of mine kept the Sportsmans Arms. Then again, there was a piece in the *Indicator* when Barry Brunt was the licensee. This chap Harry Clements was a long-serving licensee, starting in 1934, and the story was that when he died in 1956, the clock in the bar stopped and would never go again. All the combined efforts of the local clockmakers and watchmakers around here - Craddock was one who had a go at it - couldn't get it to start again. I heard other bits and pieces.

Now, to get to my part of it, just before I took over as licensee of the Sportsmans Arms, the previous incumbents, Stan and Joan, said, 'You will see the ghost'. I replied, 'Oh, I've heard about this ghost and it's Harry Clements isn't it? I have heard about it from the late Barry Brunt and other licensees'. She said, 'Yes, but don't worry, you won't get any scares, it's benign. It's not a malicious thing, it's a friendly ghost'.

Anyway, I put it out of my mind. After I had been there about a fortnight or three weeks, early one morning at about a quarter past eight (I always started at seven) I looked through the lounge over the bar and a chap was sitting down there. How a ghost can sit on a physical seat I don't know. I said, 'I'm sorry mate, I don't know how you have managed to get in, but we don't open until ten'. And as I said it, the chap just faded away. I thought, 'I'm going barmy here', but I'd already seen a couple of pictures of this Clements and I realised that it was the sort of thing I'd heard about since the 1960s and that manifested itself from time to time. The apparition was medium height with black hair, it had got a white shirt on down to the cuffs, a black waistcoat, black trousers and I think it had a watch chain. These clothes were like a uniform with the licensees, in those days, the barmen had to look smart. There was none of this lounging around in jeans that you see today. Well, as I said, he just faded away and that was the first I realised that I had seen something a bit out

The Sportsman's Arms
with an unusual customer
who pops in occasionally for
a drink

of the ordinary. It didn't vanish, like they say some ghosts vanish, it faded away right in front of my eyes. If it had gone suddenly perhaps I would have thought I'd had a drop too much to drink - although I never drank at work. I have seen too many people go bankrupt with that nonsense.

If I had seen it just once I would have thought I was going barmy but I saw it too many times. I would say that the next time was some six months later and that was in the bar. It just stood there. It wasn't looking at me at all, it was just staring. It faded away after about 20 seconds. It was there just long enough for you to have a good look at it but it didn't hang about. That time I was ready for it and it didn't bother me at all. It wasn't a frequent visitor. I would say that I saw the apparition probably about ten times in the first four or five years I was there.

The cellar was a good, deep underground room and I spent a lot of time in there because I was in the *Good Beer Guide*, I always kept cask ale and I wanted to make sure my beer was up to standard. The cellar is your workshop. You spend most of your life down the cellar creating the beer. It's hard work keeping the customers. Many a time I would feel that somebody was watching me. I felt that the apparition was keeping an eye on me to make sure that I did the beer-making correctly as I was using old fashioned methods.

I never saw it in the cellar but I felt its presence there time and time again. Something was there and it was tangible. You could have reached out and touched it. Many a time I swung round because I had several young members of staff who were a bit prone to tricks but there was never anybody there. When I got to the top I would say, 'Have you just been down that cellar?' and they would say, 'No'.

My daughter, Julia, reckons she glimpsed it once and I would say that half-a-dozen of my customers reckoned that they saw it. Pete Hopwood was the last customer in and he was waiting one night while I was clearing up. He had a habit of standing at the end of the bar so that he could see into the passageway between the lounge and the kitchen. He called me back saying, 'Paul, there's some chap just gone into the kitchen'. I said, 'I doubt it'. I went and had a look and I told him, 'There's nobody there and in any case, if he's gone round the corner into the kitchen there's only the dumb waiter and it's still there, he can't have gone up on that'. Then I had a thought, I said, 'Hang on, what did he look like?'. The answer was 'Some bloke with a white shirt and a black waistcoat'. He was giving me a first-hand description of what he saw which was exactly what I had been seeing. I said, 'You shouldn't worry about it, he's been dead since 1956'. He was adamant that he had seen somebody and he hadn't known anything about the so-called legend. I had to give him a drop of brandy.

Pete Grummet worked for me and he saw it one night. Unbeknown to me, he kept three or four customers back in the lounge. I didn't encourage stop-overs because you didn't offend anybody then. I wasn't there, I'd gone upstairs and the last thing I said to him was, 'Don't be too late'. He saw a figure come to the bottom of the stairs and turn towards the lounge. He called to his friends, 'Hayup, Paul's just come down the stairs'. When he told me about it the next morning, I said, 'It certainly wasn't me, what was the chap wearing?' and he said, 'A white shirt with a black waistcoat on'.

Another of my staff, certainly saw it and thought it was me. I hadn't given any authorisation for a stop-back and he had kept a few customers back. He saw a figure move past the hatch and said, 'Paul's here, we've had it!'. When he told me about it the next day I asked him what I was supposed to be wearing. 'He said, 'A white shirt with a black waistcoat on. I thought you looked a bit of a toff.'

Then my family smelt fish and chips in the living quarters at a certain time every Friday night. The smell couldn't have wafted in because there was no fish and chip shop next door by then. I must admit that I only smelt it once because I didn't spend much time in the living quarters; when the pub was open, I didn't have time. The story has it that the Clements family bought fish and chips every Friday night from Len Thomas's next door and settled down to eat them. Previous licensees have said that you can smell these fish and chips.

In 2001 we had major refurb. In the lounge was a huge ornate fireplace of marble and wood. It was the central part and at the back of it were two pillars which were holding the building up. When they took the fireplace out they had to put two hydraulic jacks in its place. I said to them, 'I hope you have got those in right because I sleep on the third floor on top of those! We must have disturbed something because I never saw that figure again.

There's absolutely no doubt whatsoever that that place was haunted, that there was a ghost. I think that every successful licensee that's been there has seen it. After that refurb it never manifested itself to me again and I never felt it was there, even though the cellar was the same, it hadn't been touched. The developers had knocked the fireplace out and a lot of the old stuff out. It was almost as if they had knocked him out as well.

It was a cracking pub, I enjoyed every minute and only left because I had a bad accident.

The Sportsmans Arms is still there, in Peakman Street, despite the new town developing around it.

Flowers for a Baby

The Redditch Development Corporation swept away the centre of the old town and replaced it by the large Kingfisher Shopping centre. When the centre first opened, it had the reputation of being haunted and strange happenings were often featured in the local press. A memorable tale comes from one of the security guards who was on night duty and had to go round keying in at certain positions every two hours during the night. He was crossing the balcony when he saw, gliding towards him, 'a guy in a robe-shaped thing'. He rushed back to the lift, pressed the button for the ground floor, looked up and saw that the ghost was in the lift with him. Happily, as the lift went down, it left the ghost behind. After that he went to work for another company.

Within a few months the paranormal incidents petered out and although an occasional story, such as the one below, comes from the Kingfisher Centre, this is no more than from any other large shopping centre. Part of the Kingfisher Centre is built on ground once owned and used by the Congregational Church in Evesham Street.

About ten years ago I worked in a Kingfisher Centre store. Every time we walked through the door there was a peculiar sensation but none of us really took any notice of it. We used to have the money and various valuables in the shop, it was a bit dodgy, especially if we had a late night opening when Mandy, a fellow employee, and I were alone in the shop, and the security guards would come to the back door to make sure we were alright. One of the guards, I think it was Mark, would come into the kitchen where we had our cups of tea but he would never walk down the shop. He would say, 'I don't like this shop' and we would just laugh it off.

I had been there about 12 months when the first unusual thing happened. If the postman came and we weren't there he had to put the post through the letter box which is very low on the floor. Mandy and I went into work one Monday morning and when we got to the door we saw that the letters had gone through the letter box and were laid out end to end right across the floor as if somebody had carefully placed them like that. We thought one of the other girls or the boss had done it as a joke so we gathered them up and thought no more about it. The next morning the same thing happened again. I phoned the boss and asked him if he had been playing silly devils. He said no, he hadn't been near the shop. Then Mandy and I went downstairs. The first floor down is the basement where the crocks and ornaments are stored and when we opened the door, it was just like opening a freezer, it was absolutely bitter. We went back upstairs rather scared.

On a glass shelf in the basement were a pile of table mats and the

Some of the shops in the Kingfisher Centre when it first opened. The Centre has now been redeveloped.

next night, as we were locking up, we heard a clatter. We turned round and we thought at first the table mats had fallen off the shelf but there again, they were laid nice and neat across the floor. By this time we were both a bit scared because we didn't know what was going on. We came home and sat and talked about it and we decided to phone up Anne Jones, a specialist in the paranormal. We phoned my boss and he said that he would like us to do a seance. So Anne and I went to the shop together with Mandy, the boss, his wife, and two other staff. We started doing this seance down in the bottom room and nothing really happened. We called it a night and went home.

About a week later I was downstairs serving some crockery to a lady, she was looking at me, talking, when all of a sudden she stopped in mid-stream. She just froze. Her mouth opened and her eyes popped. I thought she was having a fit and I asked her if she was OK. Then I noticed she was looking over my shoulder. Behind me, on the wall, were glass shelves with china and crystal on and as I turned round I saw that it was as if somebody was taking the top shelf off the bracket and lowering it gently on to the second shelf, then taking the two shelves and lowering them on to the third shelf then on to the floor. The customer ran out in quite a state.

That was when I decided we'd got to get Anne back. She came a few nights later and we went down into the cellar and we all started to talk about what had happened. Anne and I were asking if anyone was there and Anne was taking photos. All of a sudden I started to speak in a young female voice. It was my mouth speaking but it wasn't my voice coming out. The boss did tape this but whether he's still got the tape or not, I don't know. I was crying and I was saying, 'the baby's died'. Anne was talking to me like you would talk to anyone and getting me to answer questions. It appeared that this lady, Megan, had had an illegitimate baby and the child had died. The child had been buried where the Kingfisher Centre store now stands, in unconsecrated ground. Megan had died of a broken heart. She said that she hadn't got the child blessed and it wasn't buried properly. She wanted me to go to the church over the road, (we assumed that was the church on the Green) and take some flowers and she described exactly where she wanted the flowers put.

I went through her life, how she had been badly treated, and how she had been hurt, actually having the baby after a rape. We called it a night and I went home. I was in a bit of a state because it frightened me, I knew I was talking but I didn't really know what I was saying. The boss played the tape back to me the next night, which was a bit

Inside St Stephen's Church (by kind permission of the Vicar)

frightening again. On the Saturday, I said, 'I'm having half-an-hour off work, I'm going over the road to the church and I'm taking some flowers'. I bought a couple of little bunches of daffodils, went into the church and asked the vicar if it was alright if I put them near the altar and I explained why, fully expecting to be thrown out. He said that as long as I didn't do anything else it was quite alright. I have never been in that church before but I knew it so well I knew exactly where to go and what to do as if I had been there every day of my life. So I put the flowers on the altar, then I went and sat in a chair and said a little prayer for the baby.

When I got up I swear there was a woman standing at the doorway of the church. When you come into the church, there's the first door, you have the shop on the right and another door's there. She was by that second door and there was a mist around her. She was in a long brown skirt with a shawl round her shoulders - rags I suppose you would call them - and she was smiling. She was only about five feet tall, she was petite and small and she wasn't very old, I would say she was 17 or 18 at the most. You know on foggy nights, you see someone walking to you and you see the outline and then as they get closer the features become clearer, it was like that. She had red thread veins on her face - a red face from the cold, and she was very dark around the eyes as if she had had no sleep. Her hair was pulled straight back, I assume it was tied at the back because there was a little bit showing over her shoulder. I think she had dark brown hair but it was misty and I could only see the front of it. I had to walk past her and she moved to one side to let me out.

When I got back to the Kingfisher Centre store, we went back down into the room where we did the seance, and all of a sudden the place had a nice warm feeling.

Everything was fine for about 12 to 18 months, then silly little things started happening again. The lights kept going on and off. We would hear a bang when nobody was about. I tried to talk to Megan but I'm sorry to say that a couple of weeks later we were all made redundant so I honestly don't know what happened after that.

Skipping Time - Enfield

Near the centre of Redditch is a large industrial estate, built on the old 30-acre Royal Enfield (of motor bikes fame) site. The name 'Enfield' dates back to the 1890s when the company went bankrupt and was under new management. The first order to put them on a sound financial footing was for gun parts for the Royal Small Arms Company in Enfield in Middlesex, so to celebrate, the company named their next bicycle 'The Enfield'. The word Royal was added the following year. Round the edge of the Enfield estate are a number of late Victorian three-storey houses. Victoria*, her husband and small son, moved into one of them in 2004.

Our son was eighteen months old at the time. Like us, he slept in a bedroom on the middle floor. On the top floor was the guest bedroom which we found very difficult to heat, no matter what we did it always seemed icy cold.

Both my husband and I do shift work and sometimes we would go and sleep in the guest room where it was quiet. We both felt we were being watched, and it wasn't a nice feeling. The room felt hostile.

On the middle floor we could hear a thud, thud, thud, almost as if someone was running about, especially when I put my son to bed. The thudding would go up to the top floor, across and down again, it was really noisy but it always stayed on the top and middle floor, it never came downstairs.

I was on the top floor one day, changing the bedding, when someone came up behind me and hissed in my ear. I thought it was time to get someone in.

We brought in someone from the Spiritualist Church. She said there was a man there who was extremely agitated because he was looking for his daughter who had died and he couldn't find her. He felt that

Housing opposite the old Royal Enfield site.

we were in his house and he didn't want us there. He felt that we were interfering. She did a little ceremony and the problem went. We do feel that he comes and goes occasionally but not very often.

The fascinating thing was that she gave us the name of the man, and because we own the house we were able to look at the deeds. It was the name of the person who first lived in the house when it was built in the 1900s.

We still had the running about on the middle floor but we weren't bothered about that. Then we had some friends from Bristol to stay. I didn't say anything to them about the noises but our friend said to us, 'Did you know you have got a little girl skipping round your house?'. When we thought about it, that was the noise we were hearing, it was a curious thud, thud, thud, just as if someone was skipping.

She told us that the little girl had a basket of sea shells she had been given as a present and she had given one to our son. The strange thing was, that when our son was eighteen months old, I had found a polished seashell in his cot. I'm a very finickity person, I know exactly what I have got and where it is but I didn't know where this seashell had come from. There was no way our friend could have known that.

Our friend said that the little girl was grounded here and she would send her home. We haven't had a problem since.

The Prophecy - Batchley

Adjacent to the Enfield estate and on the western side of the town is a mix of woodland, playing fields and houses known as Batchley. The brook from which the area takes its name was known in early medieval times when it powered a whole series of mills and was used by the monks of Bordesley Abbey. The Batchley Estate was begun in 1933 and enlarged over the years. One of the houses is occupied by Molly*, who finds her ability to predict the future rather embarrassing, so it was her mother who told us about it:

My daughter, Molly*, can see what's going to happen in the future. She knows she's got the ability but she's very shy about it. Her son will be here and she will say to him, 'If you do that you will be hurt' and it's something quite harmless that wouldn't normally hurt him. He's got a strong will and he will go and do it and I bet you £10 to a penny he'll hurt himself just as his mom said.

My son is in the army, he was doing his training for parachute jumping and he didn't tell us until he was nearly ready for the jump. I said to Molly, 'Your brother is going to do a jump within the next fortnight'. A couple of nights later he was home on leave, and she said to him, 'Don't do the jump'. He asked her, 'What do you mean?'. Her reply was, 'I know it's daft but I dreamed last night we were visiting the hospital and your ankle or something was smashed'. His reaction was, 'Oh yes, yes'. He really doesn't believe that she can predict the future and he thinks it's funny. At that time he was living in Batchley with his girlfriend and a couple of nights later the girlfriend phoned me up. She said, 'You know your stupid son, the cat got stuck up the tree, your son climbed up the tree, got the cat out, got halfway down the tree, slipped and smashed his ankle'. My daughter had seen him with the broken ankle but it was nothing to do with the parachute jump.

Sometimes her friend, Mandy, goes to work on the bus and sometimes in the car. My daughter phoned Mandy and told her not to go to work in the car. She said, 'I had a dream last night and your car was all mangled at the front'. Well, Mandy is like me, sometimes she takes notice of Molly's warnings and sometimes she doesn't, it depends what mood she's in. Mandy says she got into the car, turned the engine over and thought, 'Molly is having one of her funnies again, she has warned me not to go in the car so I'll go on the bus this morning, it won't hurt'. So she left the car at home.

She had only been at work for three hours and the father phoned. He said, 'We've had an accident but don't worry we're all OK. My car wouldn't start this morning. Your car was on the front so I used that and I'm sorry, a car has hit me and taken the front of the car off'. He had smashed all the front of the car in, exactly as Molly had seen.

I ride an electric bike, it's a light bike, there's not a lot of weight to it and it goes about 15 miles an hour. About five months ago she came in on the way to taking her little boy to school and she said, 'Mom, be careful how you go to work. If you hang on, I'll take you'. I said, 'You won't be able to take me until twenty past nine and I've got to be there for nine. I'll be alright, I've been riding now for three years'. I was on my bike and I was just by the garage on the left hand side as you go towards Alvechurch - I had just got past the golf club when my back tyre blew. I went across the road and I missed a lorry - I swear by only half an inch - I managed to turn the wheel and I went back, hit the kerb went back towards the lorry and then back on the kerb. Obviously I came off my bike then.

A man came to me and picked me up and asked if I was OK. I was so embarrassed. I said 'Oh I'm fine'. The brake cable had gone and the wheel was shattered. I was bruised all down my side.

I walked all up Grange Lane and on to work. I phoned my daughter and said, 'Before anybody tells you, I've had a bit of an accident but I'm fine'. She picked me up on the night and brought me home, she told me, 'Mum, I knew something was going to happen I told you not to use your bike'. I asked, 'What do you mean?'. She said, 'I woke up

Batchley pool, at the heart of the Batchley estate.

in the night and I was shouting, mom, mom, mind the lorry!'. Now I didn't tell her I'd almost hit a lorry, I just said my wheel had blown, I'd gone across the road and come off on the side near to the garage but she knew exactly what had happened. I was lucky I hadn't gone under the lorry.

Romans in Redditch

The Romans invaded Worcestershire in the middle of the first century and stayed here for just over 350 years. They made such an impression here that we still feel their presence today, chiefly in the network of roads created by them. When we drive from Alcester to Studley we are following the site of Icknield Street, where legions once tramped 'their cohorts gleaming with purple and gold'. At Ipsley, the Roman road is picked up as the B4497 known as Icknield Street Drive, it emerges as a footpath through Church Hill and becomes Icknield Street at Beoley.

The Romans built a large villa and fort overlooking Droitwich, when the town was known as 'Salinae' – the place of salt. Roman roads radiate out in all directions, many of them known as 'Saltways'.

A Roman soldier

Unfortunately, we have lost the name of the contributor who gave us the following lovely anecdote:

One cold and frosty January morning a few years ago I went to see some friends. At that time I lived in Oak Tree Avenue, Batchley, and it was late morning by the time I was on my way home along Salters Lane, I was walking along, thinking about nothing in particular, when suddenly I spotted four Roman soldiers walking in file towards me. I looked round to see if there was anybody I could ask, 'Can you see that?' but nobody else was around. They looked very vivid and very solid. I couldn't bring myself to have a good look at them but I know that they weren't carrying shields or banners or spears and there was some metal glinting on them – I assume this was armour. It was a raggle taggle group. I can remember that they looked worn out and weary, they were dragging themselves slowly along and were bent over with exhaustion. They looked as if they had been walking too far, or perhaps been in a fight. They seemed like the vagabond back end.

I thought, 'I can't handle this' so I didn't look at them as they came past me and I didn't turn round to see if they went on or disappeared.

It was only later that I learned that Droitwich was a Roman Town and the salt came this way. I had no preconceived idea.

The White Lady of the Home - Headless Cross

There is nothing sinister in the name, historians say that it merely refers to the fact that a Mr Hedley lived here on the cross roads.

Near Headless Cross was once a field in which stood a barn. The tale is told that a young girl hung herself there when she became pregnant, a great scandal in Victorian times. The barn was pulled down and houses built on the site. In one of these houses, a young couple kept seeing a ghost in old fashioned clothes walking across the landing.

Next door is a Retirement Home. One of the Senior Nursing Staff reports:

Some years ago we had problems at the Retirement Home with a similar ghost that seemed to have wandered in from next door.

There were only two of us on night duty and we had to do the rounds every hour. There were only four bedrooms on the ground floor and Mrs P, who was several rooms down the other end of the corridor, would shuffle from her bedroom to the toilets, making a distinctive shuffling noise. We heard this noise one night and the other nurse said, 'It's only Mrs P coming back from the toilet'. I went out to have a look, Mrs P wasn't there but there was a white figure at the other end of the corridor. It was female and youngish but you couldn't see any details on her face, she was white, like a sheet all over. It was there for a second or two then it had gone.

That night we carefully shut all the doors along the corridor but when we did the rounds an hour later they were all open. It was very weird.

Whenever we lost a resident one of us would always see the figure. It may not be immediately after, it could be a few days later, but one or other of us would see it. It would always appear at about three o'clock in the early morning.

The retirement home is now under new ownership, has been redeveloped and has changed its name. Since that time the ghost has not appeared.

The Tragic Friend

The road from the town centre rises sharply towards Headless Cross. Many cyclists dismount and push their bikes up the hill. Margaret's friend had ridden up the hill, perhaps she was tired and not thinking properly when she had the accident:

About 55 or 60 years ago I had a friend. I wouldn't say we were bosom pals but we were both in our early twenties and we both sang in the choir at St George's Church. She lived in Birchfield Road and after choir practice she used to cycle home with a friend who lived at Astwood Bank. They both cycled up Mount Pleasant then when they reached Headless Cross her friend would carry on along the Evesham Road and she would turn into Birchfield Road.

One night, after choir practice, there was an accident, she was hit by a car and killed. The driver said she turned right in front of him.

I heard about it the following day and that night, I woke up feeling very strongly that she was standing by the bed. She said to me, 'Don't worry about me, I'm alright. When it's your turn to come, I will come and meet you'.

It didn't upset or worry me, it wasn't a life-changing experience or anything like that but I have often thought about it. I have wondered if it could have been a dream but it seemed very real at the time.

Boney's Island - Crabbs Cross and Hunt End

This is an old area of Redditch, where the main road, the Evesham Road, is lined with Victorian houses. The ground drops sharply on each side of the road, in fact this is part of an ancient and prehistoric ridgeway. It was here before the invention of the wheel and before the introduction of the horse. Primitive man would trudge along it, hoping to avoid the packs of wolves, the wild boars and the robbers.

In 1642, the first year of the civil war, Charles I is said to have reviewed 10,000 troops here on his way to relieve the siege of the garrison at Hawkesley House.

The Redditch Development Corporation lowered Crabbs Cross island by some fifteen feet, which explains the presence of a red brick wall on the one side.

The Worcestershire and Warwickshire boundaries meet near Crabbs Cross. All kinds of dubious activities were carried on at this spot, because if the local constabulary tried to make an arrest, the offender only had to step over into the next county to be outside their jurisdiction. Illegal bare fist boxing matches took place, and many a magistrate was frustrated by the assailants escaping justice by stepping over into the next county. Locals say that barefist boxing was so popular that horses and carriages stretched for half a mile in all directions, and this is why the island has the nickname, 'Boney's Island'.

The most notorious criminal in Redditch lived here, Old Crowther, who dealt in stolen needles. The story is told that Old Crowther was setting off on a burglary one night when he was met by the ghost of his wife, who had died some years previously, telling him to go back home as a trap had been laid for him.

The Strange Bedfellow

Down the hill from Crabs Cross is Hunt End. This is one of those quiet hamlets, an insignificant collection of houses and a pub, where great industries began. George Townsend arrived in the early 1800s, set up a centre for brewing beer and cider and went on to found Royal Enfield. For about ten years, cars were also made here. Royal Enfield moved to the centre of Redditch and the factory was taken over by Scott Atkinson, who was responsible for the development of a new Swedish invention, the nickel cadmium battery.

Strange happenings are said to occur particularly where there is illness or unhappiness in the house, as in the following case:

My husband and I were splitting up but we lived in the same house in different rooms. The woman my husband was going off with was horrible, she made life very difficult for us. My daughter was going through all this from when she was about 11 to when she was 15. It made her very upset.

Anything that happened, happened in my bedroom. About a month before my mother died, I saw her in the bedroom, waving her arms. My husband came home one day and he thought my daughter and I were in my bedroom talking, he could hear voices. He discovered that nobody was there. I was in the same bedroom a few weeks later and I heard voices behind me. They were whispering, a male and female voice, but they were indistinct, I couldn't catch any words. I turned round but nobody was there. I assumed it was my mother and my brother having a conversation, they both died some years ago.

After my husband had left I felt someone sitting on the bed on two or three occasions. When you sleep on your own you know whether somebody else is sitting on the bed or not! The first time it happened

Redditch

Hunt End, viewed from Crabbs Cross, in February 2007.

not long after I had gone to bed, I felt the bed go down and there was a depression in the bedclothes as if someone had sat there. On another occasion I woke up in the night to feel the weight of somebody sitting on the bed.

I once saw a little girl with blond hair standing in the doorway. When anything dramatic is about to happen in the family, such as a death or a new arrival, I see an elderly gentleman standing at the bottom of the bed. My sister and I are both a bit psychic but my daughter won't have anything to do with it, it frightens her.

Possessed Ballerinas - Oakenshaw

Oakenshaw, Woodrow and Greenlands are all adjacent to each other on the southern side of Redditch, and all are new developments created by the Redditch Development Corporation. Oakenshaw and Woodrow are named after farms demolished to make way for the new town.

Mike moved into a new house in Oakenshaw in 1987.

The house was only 3 years old but from the day we moved in,

97

very often I would come home, walk through the door – there was a balustrade landing – and it was deathly cold. It would be so cold that the hairs on the back of my neck would go up. And you would feel eyes peering straight through you. It didn't happen every time, just now and again. I was sure there was something in that house. We would tell people and they would never believe us.

One Saturday evening friends came round for dinner. We ate our dinner then we went into the lounge and sat having a coffee. Suddenly, the room went deathly cold. You could have cut it with a knife. The dog was sitting by me, his ears went flat, his hackles rose, he put his tail between his legs and hid under the coffee table.

We had a wall unit on which we had four or five wind-up ornaments, ballerinas and such like. We hadn't played them for a number of years and we hadn't wound them up. Suddenly, the lights went dim and every one of those ballerinas started to go round and play a tune. When the last tune had finished the lights got brighter and the room went warm again. My friends said, 'What the hell was that?'. We all looked at each other, we were just gobsmacked. That was the end of the incident. It was unbelievable. I'm glad that we had two friends in who could verify it!

We were in the house for 13 years and eventually we sold it, not because of the goings-on. While we were waiting to move, two other friends came round. All of a sudden there was a smell of burning. My friend was avid that the entire wiring of the house was about to go up. The smell was acrid beyond belief. He was frantic. He was pulling plugs out and inspecting the fuse boxes but he couldn't find anything. The smell was putrid. He even went to the mains and ripped the seal off the incoming meter to stop the electricity coming into the house. It still carried on for another 20 minutes, then all of a sudden, it went. My son is a fully qualified electrician and he came round and went through the house with a toothcomb and he said, 'Dad, there's nothing wrong!'.

A few days later the same two friends were in the house. The two wives were downstairs and my friend was with me in the little back bedroom which is my study and is where I have my computer. My wife called up, 'Would you like a drink?' and she went to put the kettle on. He was standing in the doorway and a few minutes later I heard him say, 'Oh thanks, Maggie*'. Then he turned round and he was ashen. I said, 'What's going on?'. He said, 'Somebody has just pushed me and I thought it was your wife bringing me a cup of coffee'. This guy was six feet seven inches and not one to be easily

The spooky Oakenshaw Spinney. There are strange happenings in a nearby house.

frightened. We left a week after that.

Now I don't believe in flying saucers but if one landed in my front garden then I would believe in them. That was an experience I shall never forget, I remember it as if it was yesterday.

Behind the Fireplace - Woodrow

If anyone can explain the existence of the photograph in the following story, do let the publishers know. The address is in the front of this book.

Four or five years ago I was living in Astley Close on the Woodrow estate. I was just passing through the hall when, about ten or twelve feet away, I saw a little girl walk out of the wall and go right through the stairs. I only caught a fleeting glimpse of her but she was whitish all over as ghosts are supposed to be. She was a very British-looking ghost, aged about 12 and, I would think, about 5 feet 7 inches tall. Although she looked fairly solid, you could see through her.

I was chatting about it to the family in the evening and my partner said, 'Oh I think I have seen her' and my daughter said, 'I have seen her as well'. That was three of us had seen her, all independently and all when we were on our own.

A few months later we decided to change the fireplace. Although it was a fairly modern brick fireplace we didn't like it. When we pulled the fireplace out we found, behind it in the wall, a photograph of a young girl. Now whether this was the girl that we saw or not, I couldn't tell you as I only caught a fleeting glimpse of the ghost and I didn't study the photograph. Anyway, my partner said that it was intended to be there, so we put it back and I plastered over it. As far as I know, it's still there.

The Psychic Student – Winyates Green

On the eastern edge of the town is another of the Redditch Development Corporation's housing estates, Winyates Green, built round Ipsley Alders Marsh Nature Reserve. In one of the smart new houses lives an interesting young lady in her late teens, she is a student and lives happily at home with her parents:

Wherever I go I get a feeling about something or see something.

We have been in this house for three years. The most vivid thing occurred just a couple of months after we moved in. My mum was showing a friend of hers round the house. We went into my mum and dad's bedroom and I moved into the room, mum and her friend were standing in the doorway. There was a mirrored wardrobe and when I looked in the mirror, behind my mum's friend there stood a man. He was in his mid-thirties, he was wearing blue jeans with a blue striped jumper and he had dark hair. It was as clear as if he was a real person. I said to her, 'You have got a man behind you'. I looked back in the mirror and he had gone.

We bumped into the couple we bought the house from and my mother asked them if anyone had died in that house answering the description. The woman said that nobody had actually died in the house but her brother had died from a brain tumour shortly after working on the extension, which was my mum's and dad's bedroom. She showed me a photo of her brother which was very similar but I don't know if it was the same person.

At the bottom end of our kitchen I'm always seeing a man in a black pointed hat and robes, not every time but often. He is as clear as day. His hat is covering his face. He stands there with his head bowed and his hands together and he doesn't move. He's always in the corner of the kitchen. I can often see a black figure walking through the house especially round the kitchen and dining area. He doesn't seem to have a nice feeling which is strange considering he is a monk.

For some weeks, my mum was going to Ragley Church, but she wouldn't tell me where she had been. Then one day, she said, 'You can come with us'. She didn't tell me anything about it but the night before we went I was able to describe precisely where we were going. I said that there was a gravel drive, a bungalow-type building which was old and covered by trees, a big evergreen, and behind it woods and houses buried in the wood. And there was a great medieval church.

We hear a lot of heavy, slow footsteps. Doors lock and unlock themselves. I can lock a door and 10 minutes later it's unlocked. You switch a light off, walk out of the room and the light is on again.

In our last house we had a lot of trouble with things going missing. I was sitting in a chair and I dropped a bracelet, I bent down to pick it up and it had disappeared. We never found it. You would put something down and turn round and it would have gone or be in another room. We heard the slow, heavy footsteps there as well and you always felt you were being watched.

Fluid that Flew - Alexandra Hospital

When Redditch became a new town, it was obvious that Smallwood Hospital would be unable to cope with the increase in population. The building of a new hospital was outside the remit of the Redditch Development Corporation but they did what they could to pressurise the government into providing one. The Corporation had left the town by the time the Alexandra Hospital was opened, but as a parting gift they donated a sculpture, 'The Family' which is on the outside wall by the entrance. The hospital was opened in 1986 by Princess Alexandra.

Although we usually don't print hospital stories, the relevant ward has now been completely changed so that patients can rest assured that the white form at the bottom of their bed is a hospital employee.

Ward 5 used to be the Elderly Care Ward and the ladies were six in a ward. I was a nurse there. When we first moved in all kinds of things happened. We had bags of IVF fluid flying off the shelves.

One patient kept saying 'Tell those two men to stop fighting. I don't like it'. She said they were fighting with pickaxes and swords. I thought she was going senile, but the other nurses told me that it happened quite regularly, patients often complained that they could see men fighting.

The girls on nights often saw a black cat but when they thought they had cornered it, nothing was there. We had to get the vicar in to bless the ward.

It's now the General Medical Ward and since it changed we have had no more problems.

A Haunted Honeymoon

One cold and wet winter's morning just before Christmas 2006, a middle-aged couple visited the Hunt End Books stall on Redditch market. Judith lives on Church Hill and said that thirty-three years ago, when she and her husband were on their honeymoon, her husband saw a ghost. She didn't see it as she was asleep but she persuaded him to talk about it. This is his story:

We were staying in an old coaching inn just before you get to Oxford but out in the country. I can't remember the name of it and I've often tried to trace it but I haven't had any success. We had the four-poster bed in the Queen Anne room.

The only entrance to the room was through a big old-fashioned door made of a hard wood and there was a massive bolt on the inside. During the night a shaft of light fell on the door and a young man walked through. He was about thirty with dark curly hair and very well-dressed in a Victorian or Edwardian suit with a paper collar. He walked across the room to the far side and disappeared. I wasn't really bothered. Being half asleep I thought it was probably a guest who had lost his way and wandered into the wrong room by mistake. It was only in the morning that I realised this was impossible.

STOURPORT-ON-SEVERN

hen the civil war raged through England, Stourport was just a sandy waste. It was not until 1765 that James Brindley arrived with the idea of building a canal which would run halfway up England, from Bristol to the Mersey, and he chose Stourport for the place where the Staffordshire and Worcestershire canal was to join the Severn. The canal and basins are still there today, basically as Brindley designed them. Brindley was in ill-health when he caught a chill in 1772 and never saw his dream town completed.

In 1862 the trains arrived. It brought holiday-makers from Birmingham and the Midlands and became a great recreational centre. In 'Stourport-on-Severn, a history of the town and the area', a long-term resident paints a colourful scene:

'Dad would get plastered and the kids would get pop and crips. When they returned to the railway station it was a sight to behold. The kids were tired out, mother was at the end of her tether, father very grumpy. And the young men fought over the girls just as they do today'.

Although the trains fell under the Beeching axe, the town still has a holiday air, with permanent fairs and entertainment for both childen and adults. However, the local fish and chip shop now also offers Indonesian cuisine and instead of barges full of coal, sugar and other goods the basins are crowded with pleasure craft.

A Mysterious Force

The following was told at a Kidderminster meeting in February 2007 by a gentleman who wishes to be known only as Bill. He has a friend, Philip Hartley, and Philip was one of three partners in the Stourport Marina. Unfortunately, one of the partners died, and Bill says:

The deceased partner's boat remained in the marina while the legal issues were resolved. There was nothing controversial, there was no ill-feeling but the other two partners and the widow were trying to resolve the disposition of equity.

Anyone going into the deceased partner's boat commented on the cold atmosphere, so much so that the men in the Marina wouldn't go into the boat. It was decided to move it and a crane was brought in but couldn't lift it. It was a 25-ton crane and the boat only weighed 5 ton but when the crane tried to lift it the warning bells rang and the siren came on, meaning that the boat was too heavy.

A few months later the matter of the partnership was resolved

Stourport-on-Severn

satisfactorily, The men brought the same crane back and this time, the crane lifted the boat out of the water with no problem at all. It was said that some mysterious force had been holding it down.

The Night Visitor

Lombard Street is so-called because Brindley was hoping that it would become as important as Lombard Street in London. The Workman's Club began in about 1890 as an offshoot of the Stourport Reading Society. At first it met in the Outback Pub in Lombard Street but then, in 1965, it had to vacate. By putting on concerts, cabarets, gentleman's shows etc the membership was increased from 250 to 700 and enough money was raised to build their own premises. While the club was meeting in the old premises they employed a young local lady who has an interesting anecdote to tell:

I worked in the Workmen's Club in Lombard Street during the 1960s. The manager, Bert, asked if I would like to stay in the club and run it for him while he was on holiday. I said that I would. His wife said, 'Are you going to tell her?'. He answered, 'No'. 'Tell me what?' I asked. He replied, 'You will find out. It's nothing serious, nothing to be frightened of'. I didn't bother any more and forgot about the conversation.

The Workman's Club was a very old place and quite dangerous in places. It was a three-storey building but we couldn't use the room on the first floor as you couldn't walk into the middle of the room. The floor was unsafe. I slept on the top floor and my two daughters slept in the next room.

I took the money and each night, I would put it in the money box and take the box up to the top floor with me. The first night, I heard footsteps several times. I thought I had not locked up properly and had let somebody in, but when I got out of bed and went to investigate, nobody was there. Another night I woke up hearing heavy footsteps coming up the stairs, up to the first floor then on up to my floor. I thought, 'My God, it's somebody after the money'. Then, through the door came a man. I could see him clearly. He was wearing a tweed jacket with a belt at the back and his trousers were the jodhpur type. I would say that it was an old 1800s-type dress.

He stood there for a few seconds, then he walked slowly over to the bed, bent down and picked something up. It looked heavy. Then he turned, went out and back down the stairs. I saw that three times.

When Bert came back, he said, 'Has anything exciting happened?'. I told him about the ghost. His wife looked at him and said, 'She's describing the man exactly the way you saw!'. He had seen the apparition but his wife hadn't seen anything.

There is still a Workman's Club but it's not in the same building.

Let Your Next Move Be Ours

The next story was told by John from Stourport on Ed Doolan's programme on Halloween 2006, and Ed has kindly given us permission to use it. If anyone can throw any light on the story please get in touch with the publishers. Was there ever such a company as Smith's removals, working in that area?

I don't believe in ghosts as such but this happened to me way back in the 1960s when I used to be a long-distance lorry driver. I was coming down from Scotland and I had to make a delivery further north of England on the old A6. There was a big removals van in front of me and he was only doing about ten miles an hour. This would be about five or six o'clock in the morning, early. I can even remember the slogan on the back, it said, 'Smith's Removals, Let Your Next Move be Ours'. He was going so slow that I overtook him. As I went to overtake him and went alongside, I glanced across and this man gave me a very slow cold look. He did look weird, he was very pale and he looked sad. I overtook him, looked in my mirror and pulled back into the nearside of the road. Nothing was there and there was nowhere where this van could have pulled off the road. I had to stop later on because I felt terrible.

HARTLEBURY AND THE CIVIL WAR

Stourport-on-Severn may have escaped the Civil War but the bishop's castle at Hartlebury, a couple of miles to the east, was heavily involved. At the beginning of the war, in 1642, it was turned into a Royalist garrison under the Sandys family. Three years later the garrison was strengthened and men were impressed from the neighbourhood to work on the defences. The Royal mint was there, churning out coins to support the war effort. It was never captured but surrendered when it was obvious that the Royalist cause was lost. Colonel William Sandys was then governor of the castle and in the terms of surrender he was able to walk free and keep his estates in Ombersley.

In July 1648, two years after the end of the first civil war, the Parliamentarian governor of Hartlebury began to suspect that something was wrong in the district. A search was made at Wolverley and half-a-hundredweight of gunpowder was found in a cornfield. A certain Major Harcot was arrested and brought to Hartlebury. After being tortured by having lighted musket fuses applied to the soles of his feet, he confessed all. The illegitimate son of the Earl of Dudley, Dud Dudley, was planning an uprising.

Dud Dudley is better known for his research into the use of coal instead of charcoal for smelting iron, but that was only one part of his life. He was an ardent Royalist and fought for Charles I but when the war ended in 1646 he went underground and began to raise a secret army. Major Harcot revealed that men from Staffordshire were being drilled in Boscobel Woods.

The Parliamentarians surrounded, attacked and captured them. Dud and some of his fellow-conspirators were imprisoned in Hartlebury Castle, then stripped almost naked and taken to Worcester prison. Dud managed to get on to the roof of a neighbouring house and escaped across the roofs. He was captured and sent to London to be shot. The day before his execution he managed to escape again and although he was injured he managed to get to Worcester. His wife and children had gone, his house had been sold and his ironworks destroyed. He heard his family had gone to Bristol and with great difficulty, and after many adventures, he managed to rejoin them.

He died in 1685 and is buried in St Helen's Church where there is a magnificent memorial to him.

UPTON-ON-SEVERN

n the late 1600s and the 1700s, when the river Severn carried an immense volume of trade to and from Bristol, Upton was an important river port. Many luxurious houses and inns dating back to that time, can be found here. The famous 'Bridge Parliament' was held in Upton, when the rivermen left their huge trows at the bridge and gathered to discuss their affairs.

The present bridge was built in 1938 when it replaced a bridge of 1853. The original bridge survived for many centuries except that it lost one arch before the Battle of Worcester of 1651. There's an interesting tale about it:

In the August of that year, the Royalists had been in Worcester for about five days and Major General Massey had been left to hold Upton-on-Severn with a force of 300 soldiers. One of the arches of the bridge had been blown up and a single plank had been put across the gap, but it was a brave man who walked the plank, high above the river with its dangerous currents. The tale is told that a contingent had been left to guard the bridge, but the evening was cold, supplies were poor and the White Lion, well-known for its hospitality, proved an irresistible attraction to the soldiers who crept away from their post to enjoy themselves at the inn.

Photographs of Civil War re-enactments by Helen Lee of 'Discover History'.

107

The White Lion

During the night a small contingent of Parliamentarians left the main body of the army and went to have a look at the situation at Upton, led by General Lambert. To their amazement, there appeared to be no guard on the far side of the river. Lambert picked 18 of his best men to 'walk the plank' and get across to the other side into enemy lines. In the dim light of the early morning the eighteen began their task. At any moment they could have been spotted and fired on. Walking the plank was terrifying, so they decided to straddle it instead and get across that way. As soon as they lined up on the other side they were spotted and fighting broke out. They managed to reach the church and barricade themselves inside. The Royalists soon surrounded them, firing through the windows and shoving their pikes through the glass.

General Lambert decided to he had to rescue his men. The river a little way along was shallow and possible to ford in fine weather. Splashing through the water, partly swimming, the first dragoons managed to get across, followed by the remainder of the party. They attacked the Royalists from behind. The Royalists retreated to their fortifications but Lambert's men drove them out. Major General Massey's horse was shot from under him and he was injured in the head and thigh so badly that he found it difficult to ride a horse. The Royalists abandoned everything - their camp, their baggage, their injured - and fled to Worcester, Massey among them.

The taking of Upton-on-Severn was of great importance. The next day, a Parliamentary force of 12,000 had crossed the river and was camped on the west bank of the Severn. It cut off the Royalists from Wales and from

The Pepper-pot, the tower is a remnant of the old church.

the west, so that no further supplies, munitions or recruits could come from there. It destroyed the furthermost encampment and began the first push to move the Royalists into Worcester. It was the first major skirmish of the battle of Worcester and the Royalists had lost. This was so demoralising! Cromwell himself came to Upton to thank Lambert's men for their bravery.

The main body of the church was rebuilt but pulled down in 1937. Only the old tower, dating back to the 1300s, has been left standing. A cupola was placed on top in about 1769 so that the tower has been christened 'The Pepperpot'.

The White Lion still exists, the Georgian front is only a façade and the interior is thought to go back as far as the 1500s. This was one of the favourite hotels of the famous 18th century novelist, Henry Fielding, and it is thought that he used the setting of the White Lion for the climatic scene of his great novel, 'Tom Jones'. In the novel, Tom and the love of his life, Sophia, are occupying rooms next to each other but neither knows the other is there.

The Haunts of Captain Bounds

The White Lion has a traditional ghost, that of the infamous Captain Bounds. In his young days he was a church-going, kindly youth but during the civil war his character changed and he became cruel and wicked. Two of his three wives died soon after marriage and it is rumoured that he murdered them. One of his wives is said to have been murdered in an upper room of the hotel. He also forged the will of an old lady to get her farm at 'Southend'. The tale is told that the lady's ghost began to haunt him and he drowned himself in a pool by the causeway. His ghost then began to haunt the area and was very troublesome. The minister is said to have laid the spirit ' under a great stone' that formed part of the little bridge by the pool but it was soon loose again.

Captain Bounds lived in a large Georgian House near the centre of the town, nearby are several buildings converted into flats. A young musician and his family moved into one of them and, although Captain Bounds didn't pay him a visit, he had other strange experiences:

I moved into a flat in Upton-on-Severn and the first night I suddenly sat up in bed. A vision came to me - it was like watching a round, three-dimensional TV screen. I saw a building with a large brick arch and a couple of black men tending a horse and cart. There was nothing surreal about it. They were just ordinary men doing their work. One went into the shed and came back out carrying something, I couldn't see what it was.

The next morning, as I left the house, I looked back and realised that the vision was of the house where I was living. The building was just as I had seen it except that the archway was bricked up.

A few months later I had an out-of-body experience. Not far away lived a girl who was a heroin addict. She was about 30 and into a decline. She was big trouble and everyone used to avoid her.

One night, when I was in bed, I seemed to come out of my body. I went over to the addict's house and I saw her outside her bedroom, sitting in the corridor with her head in her hands. I said to her, 'You have got children, why are you doing this?' and I gave her a good talking-to. She said nothing. Then a couple of days later, I was cycling down the road and she came out of the phone box. I wanted to avoid her, but she shouted to me. She said, 'I did listen to you the other day and I do understand that you don't want anything to do with me, you are trying to protect your daughter. I am not going to bother you but I just wanted to say thank you for caring and talking to me and I did listen to you'.

The Labourer at School – Ripple (near Upton-on-Severn)

St Mary's in the little village of Ripple is partly medieval and visitors arrive from all over the country to look at its sixteen misericords. On the underneath of the choir seats are superb medieval carvings, twelve represent the Labours of the Month, ie one for each month showing the work to be done.

In the second year of the civil war, 1643, Ripple was the scene of a nasty skirmish. Charles I had appointed Prince Maurice as one of those in charge of the Royalist army. His cavalry had already won the fight at Powick and he had an impressive military reputation. A leader of the Parliamentarians was Sir William Waller, a brilliant commander whose name brought fear into the heart of every Royalist.

Sir William wanted to keep Prince Maurice on the western side of the Severn, so he occupied Tewkesbury and sent a detachment to hold the bridge at Upton-on-Severn, this was the only place where Prince Maurice could cross the river. Prince Maurice arrived at Upton and was surprised to find it occupied by the Parliamentarians, so he decided to attack. The Parliamentarians took one look at the Prince's cavalry, jumped on their horses and fled. They aimed to rejoin the rest of the army at Tewkesbury.

Prince Maurice left most of his army in Upton to hold the town, and set off with the cavalry in hot pursuit of the fleeing Parliamentarians. Sir William heard the news and rushed to help his colleagues. The two sides met at Ripple.

Ripple was a village with enclosures round it and a lane leading to an open field. Waller drew up most of his men in the open field at the end of the lane. He was expecting the cavalry to come up the lane, and when they did so, his men would charge. However, the cavalry attacked them from all sides and it was Waller's men that were driven into the lane. There, they were trapped. The cavalry swooped into the lane, jumping over hedges and charging into their midst. Waller came up with some fresh troops and urged his soldiers to regroup on the field. Prince Maurice charged again, this time it was a massacre. At least fifty Parliamentarians were killed.

It was a great psychological victory. The Royalist cavalry had proved once more that they were invincible and this time they had beaten the mighty William Waller. Prince Maurice crossed the Severn at Upton and went on his way to join Charles I at Oxford.

Two centuries later, in 1844, the skirmish had been virtually forgotten and a school was built in Ripple. In the 1960s the old school house went up for sale, and was bought by Joan:

The School House, where the headmaster lived, was in the middle with a schoolroom on either side. The school closed in the early 1960s at the time of Aberfan as the authorities were worried about a wall falling on the school, and we bought the house in 1967. It had two-bedrooms, we extended one of them by two or three feet and moved the door to the other side of the room. The original door led to a flight of stairs down to the kitchen underneath the bedroom.

We had been in the house for about 20 years when I woke up about four or five o'clock one morning. The bedroom was very gloomy. When the floorboards were bare, you could see where there had once been a single bed by indentations in the floorboards made by the casters. I'm certain I wasn't dreaming, but where that bed had been, I saw a man moving as if he was getting out of one side of a bed. He was tall and thin and about 60 years of age. He pulled on his coat of astrakhan or sheepskin, the fur was unusually long and on the inside it looked ragged, as if two sheepskins had been roughly joined together by hand. Then he tied a cord round his middle to hold his coat together and began walking towards me.

When the bedroom had been extended, the original wall was pushed out by two or three feet so that the head of my bed was two feet or so beyond the line of the old wall. The old door from the bedroom had been right by my head. The man came along the side of my bed, passed through the head of my bed and went out through the wall and down where the staircase had been, disappearing through the bed. He was very vivid, but I wasn't at all frightened, I just thought it was strange. That was the one and only time I saw him.

I did some research into the history of the school to try to find who it could have been. When I looked up in the old records, I saw that the last person to live there had been an oldish man, a labourer who died in about 1956. I thought the man looked very much like a labourer getting ready for work.

We moved out of the house in 1996 after nearly thirty happy years there.

WORCESTERSHIRE VILLAGES

ife in Worcestershire in the time of the Civil War must have been terrible. Worcestershire was on a direct route between Wales and London and Wales and Oxford. Garrisons and fortified houses were dotted all over the county. Even the smallest village was affected in some way. This was not a war in some distant land, but in your own home. Sometimes, a father would be Royalist and the son Parliamentarian or vice versa. Or two brothers might fight on opposite sides. While Sir Edmund Verney rode to his death as the King's standard bearer at the battle of Edgehill, his son was fighting for the Parliamentarians. Some husbands and sons volunteered, others were rounded up, usually by the Lord of the Manor. Some gentry tried to raise a force for the king while others would try to prevent it. Press gangs were made illegal in 1641 but the Royalists often descended upon unsuspecting young men and forced them to join the army.

The men of the house would disappear off to war and news was scarce. Worcestershire was usually loyal to Charles I, unfortunately, this was the wrong side. No-one knows how many men from Worcestershire died on the battlefields.

Great armies tramped to and fro across the county. Evesham, Inkberrow, Droitwich, Bromsgrove, Kidderminster, Bewdley, Alcester, Worcester all found themselves playing host to a huge force. Sometimes the soldiers were well-disciplined and sometimes not. In Prince Maurice's eyes, his soldiers could do no wrong. If they helped themselves to a few valuables here or there, they deserved it. Towards the end of the 1642-1646 war and the invasion of 1651, the army was short of supplies so wherever they went, they plundered and ravaged.

A leading Royalist, Colonel Baird, issued the following notice:

Know you that unless you bring unto me (at a day and hour in Worcester) the monthly contribution for six months, you are to expect an unsanctified troop of horse among you, from whom if you hide yourselves they shall fire your houses without mercy, hang up your bodies wherever they find them, and scare your ghosts.

The army could march 20 or 30 miles in a day. One day, they could be, say, in Birmingham and the next day at your back door. You could wake up one morning and find all your cattle gone. Or, you would hear a great hammering at your door with soldiers demanding food, money and anything of value.

Taxes were heavy to pay for the war. It is said that 50 outlaws from one parish were in hiding in Shrawley wood to avoid paying the taxes.

No-one was safe. The honest baker could have his shop plundered, or an iron mill manufacturing weaponry could be blown up by the opposing side and the workers taken as prisoners or even shot. Nowhere was safe. There were skirmishes all across Worcestershire. Reverend Baxter of Kidderminster was out on his ministerial duties when he stumbled across the Battle of Ripple.

Anyone who had anything of value hid it. There are many tales of family valuables being hidden and never found again. For example, the Berkeley family of Spetchley tell the story of the butler who took the family plate, that is, the gold and silver household utensils, and hid them under one of the elm trees in the Avenue. The butler was fatally wounded. With his last breath he tried to tell the family where he had hidden it. He managed 'plate' 'elm' and 'avenue' before he passed away. The plate has never been found.

ALVECHURCH - A Child Out of Time

Alvechurch is an old and historic village. Half-timbered houses are in abundance and medieval houses are clustered round an old square. A house was built here for the Bishops of Worcester but it was pulled down in 1780. This is where the Bishop of Worcester, William of Blois, died in 1236 when Alvechurch was hit by the plague. 'Pestilence Lane' is said to lead to the plague pit where the victims of the plague were buried.

In most large villages and small towns there often seems to be one street that has the reputation of being the most haunted. In the case of Alvechurch, this is Bear Hill. It was once the main road through the village. Numbers 1-3 Bear Hill were once the old grammar school, founded in 1663. A mystery surrounds The Old House, featured in 'Alvechurch Past and Present' compiled by Pat Davies and Lorna Sage. In 1927, the attic was opened and a baby's skeleton was seen lying in the plaster. There was tremendous local excitement. Evidently, the occupants had heard strange noises in the house which disappeared after the skeleton was removed. The Coroner's report stated that the skeleton was more than 50 years old, dating back to a time when the property had been a public house. No-one knew whether the child had been born dead or alive, so an open verdict was returned and the child was given a Christian burial. Two days later, fresh flowers appeared on the grave and so there was speculation as to whether the mother was still alive. The mystery remains unsolved to this day.

In the 1990s, a single lady moved into a 17th century house in Bear Hill. Her friend says:

The house was full of bangs and creaks, and the wardrobe doors would mysteriously open and close. Drawings would appear on the

The ancient Bear Hill at Alvechurch

walls. The first time we had a look at one of the drawings we decided it was a child's drawing of a chair and a dog.

My friend and I noticed a mark on the table and on closer inspection, we decided that it was a child's hand print. We cleaned it off, went out of the room and when we went back it was there again. While we were having our meal we could hear a noise, as if somebody was singing a nursery rhyme. Another mark appeared on the wall, the sort of drawing that you would expect from a four-year old. We didn't know whether it was the drawing of a book or just an oblong piece of paper.

We decided to leave paper about and see what happened. For a week nothing happened then a child's drawing of a train, a house and a tree appeared. We asked ourselves, 'What is it trying to tell us?'.

Outside, in the garden were two trees, the one was falling over and only held up by another tree tied across the top of both. It was a windy day and the tree fell, missing me by inches. Perhaps that was what it was trying to tell me, but why the train?

When I slept there I swear that something got into bed with me. I was fast asleep but I could feel the bed go down. I couldn't see anyone. A couple of other people have stayed in that room and they have both said that they could feel somebody sitting on the end of the bed. I haven't slept in that room since.

St Laurence's - The Visitor

Although the church was rebuilt between 1859 and 1861, the Norman doorways have been retained. Inside are several old tombs, one of the most interesting is that of a knight in the late 1300s, wearing full armour with his head resting on a pillow held by two angels.

The next narrator was born and bred in Alvechurch:

In about 1963 when I was about 13 years old, my elder sister and I were in the church choir at St Laurence's. Every Thursday evening we went to the church for choir practice. At the entrance to the church is a porch with stone bench seats inside, then you come to double doors, these open into the church. One particular night it was in the middle of winter and dark, my sister was walking in front of me, and as we walked into the porch I saw a man in a light grey suit sitting on the stone bench on the left hand side. I was a little un-nerved as it was a bit unusual for a man to be sitting there on a dark winter's night. My sister walked straight past him and through the first doors. I quickly followed and as soon as I had closed the door behind me, I said to my sister, 'What was that man doing sitting out there?' My sister looked blank and said, 'What man? I didn't see anybody'. She opened the door straight away and looked out and there was no-one there at all.

I suspect that I had seen my father. He had died when I was two years old. He looked very like the photos of him that I had seen, even down to the light grey suit that he was wearing on his wedding photos.

ASTWOOD BANK - The Ghost on Stilts

Astwood Bank, on the southern edge of Redditch, is an old village with a lively community. It still holds a carnival each year which rivals any in Worcestershire, and it supports an opera society and a number of other societies. It seems to attract artists and musicians, and perhaps the number of creative and sensitive people living there explains the fact that some of our most intriguing ghost stories have come from this village.

One of the old roads from Astwood Bank to Feckenham is a winding, country road known as Dark Lane. Bill had a strange experience there towards the end of 2006.

We have lived in Astwood Bank for 31 years and we have had dogs all that time. I take them for a walk along Dark Lane twice a day. Last

Sunday evening, at about twenty to seven, I was by Astwood Bank Club. Next door is a house called the Coach House, originally it was the stables. I went down the lane and didn't see anyone but going back up, as I approached the Coach House I saw the figure of a very tall, thin man, probably about seven feet tall, his head was level with the tops of the windows. He appeared to be bareheaded with shortish hair and I had an impression that he was about forty years old. He seemed to be carrying something - a rolled umbrella or a snooker cue in a little case, about 30 inches long.

He was lurking in the shadows, it seemed as if he was waiting for someone. He would walk a few steps this way and a few steps the other way, as people do when they are waiting. He was tall and shadowy and I thought what long legs he had, it occurred to me that he was almost like a stilt walker. As I approached he moved towards the middle of the road - I thought for a minute he was going to ask me for directions, lots of people do along there. But as he got nearer he turned away and I walked past.

He was standing against the wall as I walked past. Dark Lane isn't very wide and I was only two or three yards away. I didn't like the idea of somebody lurking in the shadows. A few yards further on I looked back out of curiosity and he had disappeared.

I was surprised that he had disappeared so quickly. There was not enough time for him to go out of sight up or down the road, and he hadn't gone into one of the houses or I would have heard or seen something - a door open, a shaft of light, voices. I thought, 'He has either gone into the Coach House, or there's an entry nearby, he could have gone down that'. I just thought, 'That's strange!'.

Another thing that was unusual, people say that dogs are sensitive to spirits. The dog is an over-friendly spaniel. When you meet anybody she will go up to them and say, 'hullo' and want to be fussed. There was no sign of recognition. She always trots over and wags her tail. She just walked past as if nobody was there.

I told my wife who plays whist at the Astwood Bank club on a Monday evening. She said 'I'll ask around'. She asked me if I'd seen his face, I said, 'No, it was in the shadows'. I told her, 'Be careful what you say, I don't want anyone to think I'm a lunatic or anything. He was an exceptionally tall man, at least 6' 10" and thin'. She enquired but nobody like that had gone into the club house, it had been quiet and there were just the usual locals, all of whom were well known.

I took the dog for a walk again this Monday evening. I thought that's strange, how was he in darkness? At the end of the club house building there is an orange street light. When I walk back up past Dark Lane there is a security light. It always comes on. It didn't come on, on Sunday night. The man was in a dark area which is normally well-lit. Both of the lights were out and both of them should have been on.

In Your Dreams

One of Astwood Bank's claim to fame is that it housed one of the first communities of Baptists in the Midlands. The old chapel is still in existence but no longer used as a church. The Methodists also have an old chapel, still used as such. The Church of England St Matthias and St George was not built until 1884.

Alice* was born in Alcester but moved to Astwood Bank two years ago.

For the past nine months I have been living close to a very old chapel. Fortunately, I'm on the side away from the burial yard.

In the twilight very early one morning, at a quarter to four, I felt the hairs rise on the back of my head and I knew that there was someone in the bedroom. I was terrified. I turned on to my back and saw a man standing, looking at me. Afterwards, when I told a friend about it, she said, 'In your dreams' because the man was really quite handsome with a pin-striped shirt in blue and although I could only see down to the top of his legs, I could see that he was wearing blue jeans. He was as solid as any of us. I screamed and screamed and screamed because I really thought he was going to suffocate me and he just literally backed out of the room.

I put the light on and it took me a few minutes to summon up the courage to go into the kitchen to the telephone, then I noticed that when I went into the hall, that the curtain over the door hadn't been disturbed at all. I realised that all the doors were shut as I had left them. So I thought, 'He's waiting in the lounge for me, and if I go into the lounge he will pounce on me and that will be it'. So I put all the lights on and opened the front door. I gingerly opened the lounge door and nothing had been disturbed at all. Nobody was there. I was absolutely petrified. I didn't go back to bed that night.

I had a friend from overseas staying with me who had been away for the weekend. When she came back she said, 'You need to go and see a medium'. She thought that I was extremely lucky and had had a wonderful experience but I couldn't see that at all. I was very nervous and it catapulted me into living with my boyfriend for a time which he thought was great.

When I had been living there I had had various problems. I would get up in the morning and my pictures would be tipped onto the one side, and things would go missing and three weeks later they would be found somewhere completely different. If anybody was staying with me, their articles would go missing as well.

A few months later my friend came back from overseas and this time, because I was living with my boyfriend, she was staying in the house on her own. She rang me and said, 'I've had the same experience that you had but this time it wasn't a nice apparition, it was quite unpleasant. I think you should come back and get somebody to do something about this'.

She contacted someone that she knew in Glastonbury who told us to get out of the house by nine o'clock on a certain day and she would exorcise it. She had to do a couple of exorcisms. She guessed that it was on holy ground and she said that was the problem.

I'm still quite nervous and since then I still have the kitchen light on all night and I just keep the door partly closed.

That was the end of it, or so I thought, but then about eighteen months ago a friend of mine got herself a spiritual adviser. She said, 'It's quite painless and the effects are really quite good and you ought to have a go'. So this man came up from Wales. I opened my front door and he walked in with his girlfriend and he said, 'My God, this is a spiritual highway. You have got spirits going backwards and forwards all the time. Do you want me to get rid of them?'. I actually answered, 'No', because it feels so nice in my house now and as I don't feel or see anybody around me I really don't mind. The spirits can do what the hell they like but I don't want to see anybody again'. Only today – I keep seeing things out of the sides of my eyes. I don't know whether it's imagination or what, but today, I was going out to see a friend at around 12 o'clock and when I opened the door, I saw someone push past me about my height and with blonde hair down to their shoulders. I stepped back and looked but nothing was there. Was that somebody trying to say, 'You can win some of them but you can't win them all?'.

The late Barrie Roberts, author and legal adviser, wrote:

An exorcism is the persuading of evil spirits to abandon a place or a person, and in the major Catholic and Protestant churches may only be performed by permission of a Bishop. The church believes that it is possible to persuade a spirit to move away by using ritual acts and words with a bell, bible and candle. In the case of haunted houses, if the activity is not severe, a priest will merely bless the house.

BISHAMPTON - Two Black Eyes

During the Dark Ages a Saxon Chieftain, Bissaca, settled in this idyllic spot nine miles south-east of Worcester, and gave Bishampton its name. Since that time the manorial rights have passed through many hands, for example, in 1080 the tenant was Roger de Lacy who went off to fight for William Rufus and was banished as a result. The estate passed to his brother, Hugh. Guy Pipard, in the early 1200s, overspent, borrowed money from a Jewish moneylender and lost the property. A century later the village was given to the little nunnery at Cookhill. The church has many Norman fragments and some of the best half-timbered houses in Worcestershire are in the village.

Twenty-one years ago a young couple bought a house in the village and set about renovating it:

There was an old lean-to here, we pulled that down and replaced it with an extension. The two houses were not on the same level and where we joined the old house to the new, two steps went down. After we had built the extension for about two years, my wife and I were both seeing movement with our peripheral vision. You couldn't put your finger on anything precise. The movement went up the steps and across the door. If you pointed a finger out to the side and looked straight in front of you, that's the angle at which we saw the movement.

One night, we were sitting side by side and we both turned our heads together like ducks to look at some peripheral movement. We looked at each other and said, 'What did you see?'. We had probably both been seeing it for about twelve months after the extension had been built. We often mentioned it to each other as time went past.

Then things started to warm up. We have got three linking bedrooms that run through each other. Our bedroom was the one nearest the road and our youngest daughter had the far bedroom, however, we could look straight

Right and far right: Bishampton village

down through the bedroom doorways and see our daughter in bed.

One night, I was getting ready for bed, my wife was already in bed, and I happened to look through the doorways. We had nightlights for the children and the lights were very dim but I saw a dark figure in my daughter's room. I looked at the figure and we had eye to eye contact, I remember that its eyes were very black, and then it ran across the room. I thought it was my daughter and I said to my wife, 'The little b...'s up and she's running across the bedroom'. I marched into my daughter's bedroom and she was fast asleep. You know what children are like when they're asleep, they're absolutely sound. I came back and said, 'It wasn't our daughter'.

After that – I can't remember how long – I was washing up one breakfast time, the children were at the table and my wife was also at the table next to the cupboard where we keep the cereals. My wife went 'clonk' and looked at me and went pale. She beckoned me out of the room and she said, 'I have just been pushed into the cupboards'. We didn't tell the kids, we didn't want them frightened.

Not long after that, our eldest daughter was about 15, and she was doing a dance routine in the old kitchen which was the room nearest the road. It used to be the first port of call from the road but the door has now been blocked up. She suddenly said, 'We have got a ghost. Something has just pushed me in the back'.

All this was speculation and hearsay. There might have been a simple explanation. The sightings were fairly regular but there was no malice with them. My wife and I and my eldest daughter had the impression that the movement was a 'she'. We tried to find an explanation, we thought of everything, we even ruled out car lights.

Then in 1990, we had three days of snow and power cuts. Some friends of ours had just had a baby and they were all-electric. We had alternative fuels so we invited them to come round, we camped out in the kitchen for three days and had candles round the house.

We were gathered in the lounge where there was a fire, when the visiting mother said to my wife, 'Could you spare a minute?'. They went out of the room and she said to my wife, 'I was in the kitchen and I have been talking to you for a long time, I could see you out of the corner of my eye but you weren't acknowledging. When I asked you a question and turned round' - and her exact words were - 'It wasn't you'. She had absolutely no prior knowledge that we had a ghost. We had kept it quiet because we didn't want to frighten the children. No-one knew. She was absolutely mortified and went home.

Then the real crunch came. We were sitting round the table at a dinner party. There were some friends from Fladbury, six people, three sitting opposite three. The lady next to me, Jane*, was sitting close to where my wife had been pushed into the cupboard, and two people were sitting opposite. I was conversing to all three.

The chair on which Jane was sitting suddenly went into the table. She said, 'Oh my God'. She added, 'I have just been lifted up and moved into the table. How did that happen?'. She was quite pale. Then the lady on the adjacent corner spotted a movement to her right. She said, 'Someone has just walked up those steps and into the lounge'.

There were two witnesses who had seen her pushed into the table. We all pooh-poohed it but she said, 'Look at my feet. My legs are straight out in front. How could I push my chair forward when my legs are like that?'.

We had to tell everyone that we had a ghost. The news was red hot round the village. The next day the telephone didn't stop ringing.

After that the sightings and the incidents dwindled. It went almost totally quiet for two years. The kids were doing O or A levels and suddenly it all came back and we began to see movements again. My younger daughter was at an age when we could tell her that we had a ghost. When we told her, she was delighted. She said, 'I was too scared to say that I was aware of it'. She thought it was in her room upstairs and was happy that it had been confirmed. Both my daughters cope with it, it's not malevolent at all.

It came back for a short time and we haven't seen it since.

BARTLEY GREEN RESERVOIR - The Night Shade

Bartley Green is just outside the northern tip of Worcestershire. It was a quiet rural backwater until Victorian times when it was caught up in the expansion of Birmingham. The reservoir was opened in 1930 and has the largest stretch of water within the Birmingham conurbation. Part of the reservoir was in Worcestershire until boundary changes in 1911. The source is the Elan Valley reservoir, in Wales.

As well as providing water, this resource provided inner city dwellers with a day out; they could catch a tram and enjoy the fresh air and the expanse of water.

A retired policeman, James Hollick, recalls the time when he was taking a break there late one dark evening:

This incident occurred at the dam at the end of the Birmingham reservoir. I had been up all night on duty and I was sitting on the rustic seat set in the recess of the wall. I was on duty but I was half asleep, I had been in court all day with several cases. I was supposed to be on night duty but when you had court cases, they cut into your day's sleep. Anyway, I was sitting there, I was a bit tired and all of a sudden I heard bumpetty, bumpetty, bump, four hooves pounding like mad. Then I saw the horse coming towards me. The fellow on its back was right down on its neck and going like mad. And as it approached, the noise of hooves disappeared. The noise stopped as it was going past. I couldn't understand it. I saw the horse flash past and fade into the darkness. It was pitch dark so it had gone out of sight within a few yards.

I thought, there's something wrong here. I was just flabbergasted.

What amazed me was that, at the dam end, the water was 100 or so feet deep and it came along that road.

BEOLEY - Leave Me Alone!

The village of Beoley has now moved away to Holt End, isolating the ancient church which is so picturesque that usually each spring, it holds a snowdrop day when photographers can snap the church and the carpets of snowdrops in the churchyard. Behind the church is Beoley Hall. The Sheldons were Lords of the Manor from about 1549 to 1788, and at one time one of the three richest families in England.

As a Royalist, William Sheldon suffered heavily during the Civil War. His house at Beoley is said to have been burned down to prevent it from falling into the hands of Parliamentarians. As the present building dates from about 50 years after the end of the war, this may be correct. In vain he protested that he was never in arms and never acted for the king's party except when forced, his house and estates were confiscated. An effigy of William Sheldon lies in state on his tomb in Beoley Church.

Just over a mile from the Church is an estate built by the Redditch Development Corporation, and as Beoley is the nearest church, the Vicar was called in to help a young housewife under peculiar circumstances. As the daughter was reluctant to talk, her mother tells the story:

I think there's something unusual about my daughter's house. They have been there over a year now. The man who lived there before my daughter was a druggie, he locked himself in one room and used the corner as a toilet. He committed suicide, so the police told her, I think it was his wrists he cut, and he died in the house. It was about 18 months before they could let her in because it was in such a state.

The Council had repaired the house but, before she moved in, we were cleaning it to our own satisfaction. The top of the cupboards were filthy with thick grease and I had scrubbed them, so I know there was nothing up there, I would stake my life on that. We were standing in the middle of the kitchen having a cup of tea when an old halfpence came flying off the top of the cupboard and hit my daughter on the head.

Four or five times she and her husband have come downstairs to find a really rusty old toy car from the 1950s on the carpet. She doesn't know where it has come from. She puts it on the kitchen window sill, ready to throw it out and a day or two later she thinks, 'Oh, I'll move that car', but it's not there. A couple of days later it's back in the living room on the carpet.

She says that when she goes upstairs, she can feel that somebody's around. Her little boy is nearly five and he shouts out from his bedroom sometimes, 'Leave me alone, I want to go to sleep!'. When my daughter asks, 'What's the matter?' he says, 'That man's here again mom'. He doesn't like it. He's started telling us that there's a man living there, that mom has got a man in her bedroom. I have to say that he's the plumber or the electrician or somebody.

My daughter is always moaning about the number of bulbs that go 'pop'. She's got a big telly, it goes green for a few minutes and then it will go off and it will come back on perfectly alright. She's had it checked and they can't find anything wrong with it. I tell her it's the electricity supply, well, that's what I tell her because she's a bit nervous about it.

You can hear footsteps upstairs. Although she's a semi, the side where she hears the footsteps is over an alleyway.

She turns on the tap and the water will really gush out, then it will dribble, then it comes on normally. We've had the Council out and they say that it's the pressure going up and down but I've never known pressure going up and down like that, and then right itself in the way that it does.

We asked the vicar of Beoley if he could help, he said he didn't really do that sort of thing, but he sent a young vicar down who was really very good, my grandson hasn't been frightened since.

BRETFORTON

Two or three miles East of Evesham is one of Worcestershire's treasures – the village of Bretforton with its famous public house. The Fleece was the property of the Byrd family from the 1400s to 1977 when Lola Taplin, the last member of the Byrd family, passed away, and it became the only pub in England to be owned by the National Trust. It has featured in several films such as Martin Chuzzlewit, Clarissa and Silas Marner. In front of the hearth are two white circles and a rectangle, put there in the 17th century to protect the house from witchcraft. Lola would not allow food to be eaten in her pub. After she died, some repairs were necessary and a group of workmen were called in. As it was a fine day, when it came to lunch time they decided to leave their sandwiches in the pub and go for a stroll, locking the building behind them. When they returned, the lunchboxes had been opened and the sandwiches thrown around the room.

The Fleece has now been renovated after a serious fire.

The village of Bretforton was acquired by the Abbey as long ago as 714 AD. According to the 'Victoria County History', in the late 1100s and early 1200s the tithes from the village were not always put to the good use of the Church, as the notorious Bishop Roger Norreys held an annual feast at Bretforton and squandered the rentals in luxury and drunkenness, 'spending in one day what would have sufficed many members of the Church for a whole year'.

Tales from Reverend Shawcross

The learned Reverend Shawcross was vicar of Bretforton in Victorian times and he wrote a history of the village, in which he included a section on the local ghost as follows:

Among the more accredited stories is one attached to the field upon which the present Vicarage stands, and which bears or bore the name of "Woman Close". The legend is that a woman is seen occasionally to walk about there rather early in the night, with her head under her arm. The tradition is that she was murdered here, and that, like

Hamlet's father, she is "doom'd for a certain term to walk the night." The writer will not fail to inform about it should he ever meet with this spectre.

There is also on a certain night a funeral procession seen wending its way from Weston-sub-Edge to Bretforton Churchyard. The procession is said to have been seen amongst others by John Vickeridge, a carter of the late Vicar (Rev. G. S. Morris). On this occasion Vickeridge was returning homewards late at night from Weston. On nearing the cross roads just out of this village he turned his head and observed this procession advancing toward Bretforton. He stopped; it passed him; and he followed it into our village. The procession moved on till it entered the churchyard by the usual north gateway. This observance would be about 1854. It is singular that a similar story of a phantom funeral is told at Arlingham, the first curacy of the writer. But in this case the appearance was seen approaching the old Court House from the church. This was seen by the servants and others, May 24 1757; on that day died John Yate, the last male heir of the family residing there.

The Greyhound which used to be frequently seen coming up to Bretforton from the Badsey Field Close, has not been seen of late years. What this portended our informant (Lieutenant-Colonel Morris) cannot say.

In case any of our readers should be troubled with a haunted chamber, the writer cannot forbear adding an old English remedy and recipe to exorcise the unbidden guest. Lay half-a-pound of Brimstone in an iron dish, supported by a pair of tongs over a bucket of water, the fireplace and all openings to be closed, a shovelful of burning coal put on the brimstone, the door quickly shut, and the room kept closed for six hours. This is one of the best ways of laying a ghost. ...

John Halford, a bellringer, said to a fellow bellringer, 'The next time I ring a bell I will fall down dead'. He was threshing with a flail in a neighbouring barn when he heard that a young squire, James Ashwin, had been born after many daughters. He rushed to the Church to ring the bell and dropped dead. A looking glass was procured and pressed to his face but there was no sign of breath. The squire was born on November 28th 1806 and John Halford was buried December 17th 1806, aged 58.

Stately Haunts

Less well-known and only about 50 yards from the Fleece is Bretforton Hall. It has a history which is perhaps as exciting as any other building in Worcestershire. The Hall has ten bedrooms and a four-acre garden. It stands

*Bretforton
Hall*

on the site of a building that once belonged to Evesham Abbey.
The original Hall is thought to have burned down after the battle of Evesham
in 1265. Nearly six centuries later, in 1830, the neo-Gothic Bretforton Hall,
with its embattled tower, was erected. Dr Sir Peter Guy Manners who was
knighted for his services to Cymatic Therapy arrived in the early 1990s and
established a clinic of Cymatic and Bio-Energetic Medicine, dealing with
homeopathatic remedies and a range of other treatments. He says:

The part of the house where I have my office, has incorporated the
ruins of the monks' dwelling. When I first came here, part of this room
was called 'The Store Room' and was where they used to hang the
birds up. Along the wall was a line of old stone troughs, I suppose that
was where they put the dead pigs and dealt with them. One of our
fireplaces was originally a doorway from the Abbey. The doorway
was smashed except for the top of the arch, which was rescued and
stored for many years in one of the houses opposite.

There are underground rooms all made of stone. Downstairs is a
huge wine cellar that originally had a moving panel in it. The holes for
the wine bottles have been carved into the stone. When we first came
here the cellar was full of bottles, some of them still contained wine but
it had exploded and that sort of thing and we had to throw it away. In
the cellar are two alcoves about the height of an average-sized man,
one each side of an archway. I have been told, but I don't know how
true it is, that if one of the brothers committed any sin against the
rules of the church he was imprisoned in these alcoves, made to stand
against the rear wall and an iron grating was put in front of him. He
had to stand there for some minutes or even hours, according to the
severity of his sin. Usually the brother had to remain in a stooping
position, so when he came out he was unable to stand upright and

One of the sculptures in the garden. Did it come from Evesham abbey?

so was lain on a long stone slab set against the wall to sleep it off before he said his Hail Mary's. When we came here, one of the stone slabs had been badly smashed so we had it moved but the other was intact so it has been boxed over and is still there.

We have an underground passageway. There's a trap door in the ballroom and if you lift it up, you can get down into the first part of the shaft, although I haven't been down it. The passageway goes under the floor and under the lawn outside. Set in the lawn is a piece of garden with trees and I'm told that the reason for it existence is that it covers the passageway. It used to run under the houses outside, under the road and recreation ground to a local farm, now Bretforton Sports Club, but I believe it has all collapsed after it leaves my house - you can't have a tunnel running under a road.

The garden is full of bits of rock that came from the Abbey at Evesham, rescued, I think, by the Lay Brothers and brought here when the abbey was destroyed by Henry VIII in the 1500s. Over the road were the coach house and stables for this house. They were all barricaded up and when I managed to get into them I found that it was full of boxes of stones from the Abbey. I had no use for the property across the road, I wanted a garage this side so I sold the old coach house and gave the stones away to anybody who wanted them.

The Battle of Evesham was fought in 1265 between Prince Edward, later Edward I, and Simon de Montfort, leader of the barons. When Simon was heading for Evesham he got this far but couldn't get any further because there was no bridge across the river. I have been told, therefore, that his army ended their march here and all the troops camped out in the paddocks at the back of us. Simon de Montfort slept under the Mulberry tree in the garden. It's a very old tree and survives through offshoots, how it managed to live in the circumstances that it appears to have gone through, I have no idea. Simon de Montfort had to cross the river at the next village up where there was a wooden bridge, the relics of which are still in the river.

Most of the building that originally stood here was destroyed after the battle. There is no record of this and it's only what I have been told, however we have plenty of blackened, dressed stones in the garden.

Simon, his son Henry, and most of his troops were slaughtered at the Battle of Evesham. Along a side wall in the garden is a long mound and it has been reported to us that some of the casualties of the Battle are buried there. When part of the garden was excavated for a swimming pool, breast plate, armour and three swords were found. On the other side of the wall is a mound and on the top is a cross, you can't see it because it's covered with ivy. It is, although I have no proof of it, where the monks and lay brothers who lived here were buried.

In past centuries, when they buried their dead, instead of a horse and carriage local people had a long stone slab on wheels which they pulled. We found that in very good condition stored in one of the houses that has since been demolished. I offered it to Evesham museum who took it away but we haven't seen it since. The present Hall was built in 1830. The historian, Mr Ashwin, who lived over the road. presented me with a stack of papers and information about the Hall and its history but we put them in the tower and they were destroyed by fire in about 1995.

We thought the turret or tower only had two rooms, a library at the bottom and a bedroom above it, and it wasn't until the fire that we discovered a third room between the two. It contained two marble life-sized statues, one of a man and one of a woman. The man I have rescued and he stands in the entrance corridor, but one of the workmen slipped and hurt himself and the statue as well, so the dear lady whose statue it was, departed this world. Rule Britannia was painted on the wall and as far as we know it's still there although you can't see it because we have re-sealed the room.

There was no reason why the fire started in the turret, it suddenly burst out there.'

The mysterious fire is not the only strange occurrence at the Hall. Dr Sir Peter Guy Manners admits that, when he's sitting in the old part of the building alone, he can hear someone walking on the floors upstairs. He adds, 'I don't guarantee anything is there, but you can hear it, and I can assure you that I haven't had four or five drinks when I've heard it!'

A nurse working there saw a lady in white coming down the stairs. Then an American student refused to go into the corner of the lecture room to consult the books. She said she felt there was a presence there, but nothing could be seen. A young lady from Redditch had a friend who was a doctor there and she reports:

> In September 2005, I went to have treatment from him. As I was leaving I waved to the owner's wife, Doreen, who was sitting at her desk in the office. I also waved to another lady who was standing behind her, an elderly person, I would guess her age to be around seventy-ish. She was about 5 feet 8 inches tall, of slim build and she wore clothes that were popular with elderly people in the 1960s. Her hair was short and neatly brushed back which you would expect to see on an older person. She waved back strangely as her elbow was tucked in and her arm was tight to her chest. When I asked my friend who she was, he said that Doreen was the only person in the office. The lady looked as real as you and me.

An ex-resident named Peter tells the tale:

> We left Bretforton about ten years ago and this happened before we left. A young man lived one end of the village and his mother lived the other end, so he often walked up and down Main Street. One winter's evening at about eight o'clock – it was dark by that time – he was on his way home and had just got to the gateway of Bretforton Hall which is opposite Bretforton Manor, when suddenly, out of the corner of his eye, he saw a woman coming towards him from the gateway of Bretforton Hall which was on his left. He gave a full description of her, he said that she was dressed in grey and wearing a long skirt, probably pre-Victorian clothes. She was evidently walking from the Hall across the road to the Manor. He slowed his walking pace to let her go by but in fact she walked straight through him. We said that he went freezing cold and shaking, he started to run and didn't stop until he got home. He was about six feet two and weighed about fifteen stone!

Here is yet another story:

> About 50 years ago, my sister-in-law and two friends were walking along the High Street, arm in arm, at nine o'clock in the evening. They saw a figure walking towards them. They said, 'Goodnight', but the figure didn't answer. One of the girls said, 'Blast you then, don't say goodnight', and the figure disappeared into thin air!. Afterwards they heard that Miss Randall, who lived at the big white house with the tower opposite the manor house, (probably Bretforton Hall) had died at precisely that time, nine-o'clock in the evening.

Dr Sir Peter Guy Manners and his wife have now moved to a smaller dwelling and Evesham Museum in the Almonry have claimed the statues and decorative stones in the garden.

BROADHEATH (UPPER) - The Black Orb

Halfway between the Teme and the Severn and about half a mile before the busy streets of Worcester begin, is Upper Broadheath. Four miles to the west are the Malvern and Suckley Hills and scattered between these and the Severn are a wealth of tiny, historic villages and hamlets. About three miles north of Upper Broadheath is Wichenford Court, in the 1400s it was the home of Sir John Washbourne. An invading Welsh army, led by Owen Glyndwr, was camped on Woodbury Hill in 1405. They had received some support from the French, and Sir John managed to capture a high ranking French officer, whom he imprisoned at his house. According to local tradition, Lady Washbourne fell madly in love with the prisoner and when Sir John was called away, she tried to seduce him. He rejected her advances, so she gave him a sleeping draft laced with poison. Filled with remorse, she still wanders the site, cup in one hand and dagger in the other.

The great composer, Sir Edward Elgar, was born at Broadheath. His birthplace is now a museum administered by The Elgar Trust, containing his manuscripts and personal effects.

In the summer of the year 2000, Roger had been to visit a friend:

I was on my way home driving through Upper Broadheath at about 11 o'clock at night, when I happened to notice a courting couple sitting in a car. They were in front of a gate leading into a field not far from Laylock's Nurseries.

As I approached, my headlights picked up a black cloud five or six feet in diameter on the right hand side of the road. It was a five foot sphere but not perfectly round. It went behind the car, through the gate and disappeared. I thought, 'What on earth was that? Was it smoke or what?'.

I was so intrigued that the next day I went back to see if I could find the cause. I thought perhaps a farmer had been burning hedge cuttings but nothing was about and I couldn't find any explanation.

DUNHAMPTON - The Leaking Well

Another hamlet in this lovely area is Dunhampton, about five miles from the edge of Worcester going north along the A449. A few years ago, the licensee was a charming lady, an identical twin, named Diane:

The people who had the Leaking Well before us, Colin and Gill, decided to extend it. During the alterations they found a real old well in the garden and they made it into the main feature of the pub.

It was a really old pub and creaking all the time. The older part was a flat and every time I walked in there I felt really scared, it was quite creepy.

The weirdest thing happened late one evening. The restaurant (it had a large restaurant) was closed and all the lights were off and the back door was locked. I called to my assistant, 'Will you come down? I have to cash up now'. So we were both down at the till, cashing up. Nearby were swing doors into the kitchen, when you went through them they just slowly swung to and fro. Suddenly, they began vibrating very quickly, to and fro, very fast. We both just stood there with our mouths open. We thought somebody had got into the kitchen and was messing around, so we both ran into the kitchen but nobody was there. Our hair stood on end. We called my assistant's husband but he just remarked, 'It was the wind'.

On the wall was a photograph of the pub when it was first opened with a portly lady standing outside in a certain pose. One of our customers told us that he had seen an identical lady standing in the same place in the same pose.

I decided I would like to make a video of the pub when nobody was in it so I borrowed my brother's camcorder because it had got night vision. He put in new batteries for me. I only videoed the dining room and the cellar and the camcorder failed to work, the batteries had only lasted five minutes. Yet when my brother put new batteries in and tried it out, there was no problem.

We had problems with the electricity all the time. The lights kept flickering and electrical appliances kept going off for no reason. We spent so much money trying to put it right that we got fed up in the end and left.

FECKENHAM - Feckenham Folklore

About three miles from Feckenham, in Hanbury, lives Mr Thomas, who loves ghost stories. He has therefore been asking round his two local villages, Feckenham and Hanbury, for spooky tales.

Feckenham was once in the heart of Feckenham Forest, an area of nearly two hundred square miles which included over sixty villages and hamlets. The forest had almost totally disappeared by the time of the Civil War. On the south-west side of the church are the remains of a ditch which once surrounded the prison for offenders against forest laws.

Mr Thomas has had a brush with the paranormal. Some years ago, he visited Thirsk museum in North Yorkshire and touched the chair of Thomas Busby, who murdered his father-in-law in 1702. Busby was hung on the gallows in 1703, and left hanging on the gibbet for months. It is said that death comes to anyone who sits in the chair. The day after he touched the chair, Mr Thomas had a nasty experience and has still not recovered. The details are in 'Haunted Holidays', published in 2002 by Hunt End Books.

Mr Thomas's description of Feckenham ghosts are as follows:

Feckenham is a very old village indeed and it goes back a long time, even before the Domesday book of 1086. There's a Roman Road that goes through part of the village and a well-known ancient highway with the old milestones. A neighbour of mine, Geoff, told me that an old man he met many years ago said that he had seen a ghostly stage coach when he was driving round Berrow Hill late at night, and it startled him. Older folks will remember Berrow Hill, it's where motor bike scrambling took place in the 1950s and 60s.

To the north of Feckenham is an old pub, The Brook Inn. If you go there on a moonlit night you might see a Cavalier riding his horse from the Brook Inn to Callow Hill. He disappears in a cloud of mist when he gets to the crossroads. I heard that suicides and witches are buried at cross roads.

Someone told me that he was camping at the back of the Brook Inn with his mates when they heard shouting and a clanking sound like armour in a nearby field as if a Civil War skirmish was taking place but when they looked nobody was there.

In 2005, the licensees of the Brook Inn, Louise and Andy, complained that cups jumped off shelves and smashed on the floor, articles went missing and customers dematerialised. A full report was in 'Ghosts, Murders and Scandals'.

A much-copied photograph of The Brook in Victorian times.

FLYFORD FLAVELL - The Boot, the Dairy and the Poltergeist

The village is just off the A422, halfway between Worcester and Alcester. Six hundred years ago a church was built at Flyford Flavel but in 1883 William Laslett of Abberton Hall paid for most of the church to be rebuilt. Some Norman parts, such as the tower and the font, are still there. The Boot public house is well-known, and one or two strange stories come from there, such as the following:

About ten years ago my wife and I went for an evening meal at The Boot. We were sitting there, eating our meal when suddenly, a marigold flower dropped from nowhere and landed in my wife's dinner! We looked up but there was just the plain ceiling above our heads. There was nowhere it could have come from. I told the licensee but he didn't seem at all surprised. He said that strange things were always happening there.

A conversation with the licensee's daughter at that time, Maxine, reveals more:

My parents, Pauline and Mick, owned the Boot from 1986 to 2000. Various strange things happened there. About three times I saw a shadowy apparition standing in the corner of my bedroom. It was that of a young man and it was in the same place each time.

We had no end of problems with the electricity. We would be in the middle of a busy evening, cooking, when the electricity would go off and no amount of fiddling about would get it to come on again.

Maxine's father Mick, says that he once saw a ghost at the Queen's Head, Cubbington, but he never saw or felt anything at The Boot. It was his wife Pauline, and his two daughters, who had all the experiences. This is his wife's story:

When we first got there one of the rooms was all closed up. We opened it and found it was the old dairy. When I say 'dairy' it wouldn't be what we think of as a dairy today, it would be where they hung the hams and the sides of cattle. It was more of a cold store. That part of the house goes back to the 13th century. It doesn't look very old from the front but the back is very old. In the packing behind the Beer Engine down the cellar we found a letter going back to the time of the turnpikes.

When we opened the dairy up we made it part of the pub and the room above it was our bedroom. Often, in the middle of the night, we could smell bacon cooking. It wasn't a faint smell, it was a really, really strong smell.

We got so used to peculiar things happening, we just didn't bother. A customer would say to us, 'I have just seen what I thought was somebody going through there but when I looked nobody was there'. Silly things would go missing, little personal items. You would put them down and they would disappear, pens and things. We never found them.

We could hear footsteps going up the stairs. It was our personal living space up there, as well as the safe and other valuables. The way the stairs were situated was that you came up from a corridor then turned right at the top to get into our private lounge. Because it was a public house anybody could come up the stairs. It was very annoying,

Far left: the award-winning Boot Inn at Flyford Flavel
Left: The old diary, which has been opened up to form part of the restaurant.

135

because I would be sitting in the lounge in my precious time off and I would hear footsteps coming up the stairs. I would have to get up immediately to see who it was and nobody would be there.

As my daughter says, we always had a problem with the electricity. The pub was rewired two or three times. The electrical engineers told us the supply wasn't sufficient to cope with the electricity we were using but although we had it upgraded we never really solved it completely.

Both my daughters are a little clairvoyant and perhaps they see things that others can't. Although my one daughter always felt comfortable in her bedroom she never thought that she was on her own. She sensed that the young man that she could see in her bedroom was very irate and he would jump up and down as if he was cross about something.

Don't get me wrong, the whole building was a lovely place and we were very sorry to leave it. We felt that it was 'their' house and we had been invited into it. They were not mischievous at all except for the few items going missing. The Boot had gone through a transition period, where it had changed hands quickly two or three times. We were really interested in it, we loved it and we were there to stay. Whether it was this fact, or whether they knew that we loved it as much as they did, I don't know but they made us very welcome.

The present licensee adds:

The only weird thing that has happened since I have taken over is that we bought some little glass vases to put flowers in, one for every table. The ghost is supposed to be in the dairy and we have four tables in there. Two of the glass vases in the dairy suddenly shattered for no reason.

HAGLEY - Mourning Glory

Hagley is just inside the Worcestershire border, on the edge of the Black Country, but has managed to remain a green and pleasant village. Here is an incident with a dream-like quality, except that the young lady concerned could not have been asleep as she was working in the garden.

My father died in 1980 when we were living Hagley way, along the road to Worcester. He was very fond of the area and often walked along the fields next to our garden. A short time after he died, I was working in the garden, standing on the path, and something made me look across to the field. There I saw a golden cloud with orange lights, and in the cloud was a figure that I assumed was my father. The cloud and my father slowly rose up skyward until they disappeared.

When I went into the house I mentioned it to my mother and she said she had had a similar experience when her father died. However, one of my aunts told me off, she said, 'Your father is not up there, he's down here'.

It really did happen. It was as if he was being taken up to heaven. I was so upset about it, I cried. I just couldn't get over it.

HANBURY - Gallows Green

Although only a straggling country village, Hanbury attracts thousands of tourists. It has Hanbury Hall, the Jinney Ring (one of the best centres of arts and crafts in the county), wonderful beech woods and a medieval church set on a hill. The arcade of St Mary's is no later than 1210 and the earliest Vernon monument is nearly 400 years old.

We first met Mr Thomas, our intrepid collector of ghostly tales, in Feckenham. Here are more stories from Mr Thomas's collection:

The old Roman saltway from Droitwich to Alcester goes through Hanbury and Gallow's Green. Way back, in time gone by, an old tollhouse stood at the end of School Road. Inbetween School Road and Goose Hill Lane were the old gallows, where law-breakers from the Forest of Feckenham were taken and hanged. They were left hanging for months on the gibbet. Afterwards, the crossroads were named 'Cross-in-hand'. You can see the Malvern Hills in the distance on a clear day from that spot.

Hanbury Church

Gallows are often haunted locations and it is advisable to keep away from them at night. Many cars and motor bikes have crashed there and all kinds of vehicles have broken down – buses, lorries, tractors, cars, motor bikes. Some of them have mysteriously caught fire. Gypsies are too afraid to stay in the layby near the cross roads at night time because of the spirits.

When I have gone past the spot on my bicycle at night, I have seen dark shadows moving about and I get the feeling I am not alone. It gives me the shivers.

One of my neighbours, John, told me that his wife and son were driving along late one night passing Gallow's Green, when they both saw a horse and carriage going along the road in front of them. John says that it startled them so much they were shaking like a leaf.

Another of my neighbours said to me that he saw an old lady walking from side to side near the layby. She seemed to be enveloped in a mist. He was very shocked. Old records say that an old lady was hanged on the gallows many years ago, it must be her spirit.

There have been many stories about Gallow's Green from years gone by and I will expect to hear more in time to come.

Mr Thomas is correct, for here is one from Chris and her 31-year old son. Chris says that she saw the shape on either 30th September or 1st October 2006:

I had a weird experience when I was driving along the road from Hanbury to Droitwich. I can't tell you the exact spot on the road. This is the only time I have ever had an experience like this in my life and it frightened me to death. It was around 7.30 in the evening. It wasn't pitch black, you know when you are driving and you suddenly have to switch your headlights on, it was just about that time. My son was sitting in the car next to me and he saw it as well but we both described it differently.

I have driven down that road many times and I have seen many mists but this was quite different. It was a brown rounded shape, large enough to stretch across both sides of the road. It looked

The Hanbury to Droitwich Road.

138

like some sort of animal in a curled up position, it was a hunched, curled-up shape and narrowed towards the left-hand side. You know when deer are going to leap, they are all hunched up – the shape was like that. I didn't see the head. There was a blue and white mist round the top of it. I went cold from head to foot. It seemed to me as if the car was going along and I wasn't driving, I was looking down into the car, watching myself driving. I like to drive 50 mph along that road and I was probably going that fast but it seemed to me as if I was only doing ten. I couldn't go fast enough to catch up with it, but it was so close I could have reached out and touched it. It was weird. My son said, 'Are you alright mum?'. I said to him, 'Did you see anything just then?'. He said, 'Do you mean the coach and horses?'. Perhaps it could have been the shape of an old-fashioned coach.

A couple of nights after that, on 3rd October (it was my birthday) I was taking my son back and I saw a similar mist come out of the trees – a blue mist – and I thought, 'I hope this isn't going to happen again', but it went back. I tried to get my head around the event myself before saying anything. I had a look on the internet to see if anyone else had seen the same thing but nothing had been reported.

I used to live in the Black Country and nearby was a lane where many people said that they saw monks go down the path and across the road. I thought it was a load of rubbish.

This story illustrates the fact that if a number of people see an apparition, they don't all see the same thing. One person could just see a shape while another could see the details. Chris's son saw a coach and horses, could this be the same as John's in the previous story?

INKBERROW – The Executioner

Better known as 'Ambridge' in the 'The Archers' radio programme, the series was originally based on the Old Bull inn, not to be confused with the Bull's Head on the main road.

Charles Stuart, later Charles II, stayed here on his way to the Battle of Worcester. Although many places claim to have had this honour, here we have proof because he left his maps behind. They were locked in the vestry for centuries, as one vicar stated, 'awaiting collection on the appropriate Judgement Day'. They have now been passed to the County Archives.

An intriguing anecdote was recorded in 'Ghosts, Murders and Scandals' (Hunt End Books 2005). In the late 1800s, two fascinating letters were found behind a panelling at nearby Cookhill Priory. In the first letter, a woman who

St Peters Chuch, Inkberrow, where Charles left his maps before the Battle of Worcester.

lived at Inkberrow had written to the local priest, asking him to come urgently to 'shrive' her dying husband as he was the soldier who had executed Charles I. She explained that half a dozen soldiers had gathered together and drawn straws to see who would do the dreadful deed. In her second letter she states simply, 'Too late, he's gone'.

A lone phantom horseman is well-known in the village. Mr Cook, the Hanbury antiquarian, has an interest in folklore and tells the tale:

> On stormy nights with strong winds blowing, lightning flashing and rain pelting down, the dark shape of a lone rider comes over a hill near Inkberrow, his cloak billowing in the wind.

Looking round for characters to provide a source, there is none better than the unshriven executioner.

KINGS NORTON – Manic Raps and Doppelganger Cats

Until 1911, the Worcestershire boundary extended as far as Edgbaston and included Cotteridge and Kings Norton. To the south of Kings Norton is the parish of Hawkesley, which took its name from Hawkesley House. During the civil war the house was owned by a Royalist family, but they were turned out by the Parliamentarians who garrisoned the house. These garrisons were a nuisance, the occupying soldiers ravaged and pillaged for many miles in all directions. An army of Royalists arrived in 1645 to capture the garrison, the Parliamentarians surrendered and the house was burned down. There are more details in 'The Haunted Midlands', published by Brewin Books in 2006.

140

During the time of the civil war there was, living at Kings Norton, a Captain Greaves, a member of an old and distinguished Kings Norton family. He was fiercely Parliamentarian and gathered together about 300 locals who threw up some earthworks at Camp Hill. Prince Rupert and his army were marching from Henley-in-Arden to Birmingham, and his route took him along the Stratford Road when he found his way blocked by the earthworks. He knew that Greaves only had a small force and so, standing there with his army of 1,800, he sent a messenger to say that if the townsfolk co-operated and let his men quarter there, they would not suffer. The local folk had heard tales of Prince Rupert's looting army and did not believe him. They therefore refused to let Prince Rupert pass. A pitched battle ensued. The Royalist leader, Lord Denbigh was killed. These 300 local men twice repulsed the attacks of the well-equipped, well-trained army. When it was obvious that the battle would be lost, Capain Greaves bravely charged into the Royalist army to give his foot soldiers time to get away before escaping himself.

When the battle was over, the Royalists burst into Camp Hill village, killing and looting. The cavalry rode round, jumping over hedges and slaughtering anyone that they found. An ostler ran out to take their horses, he was killed. A minister was cut down in the street. Eighty houses were burned down.

The collection of ghost stories for this old and eventful village of Kings Norton has been provided by Ray, who lives and works in the area and has had one or two unusual experiences himself:

I live on the border of Cotteridge and Kings Norton, near the Wasthill tunnel. I did once read that when it was misty the ghosts of the dead canal folk could be seen walking on the water near the portal.

Not far away is Lifford Hall, where, as far back as I remember, ghosts have been reported. The Hall started as a Jacobean mill. It became a 'Hall' in the 17th century when Viscount John Hewitt, Lord Lieutenant for Ireland bought it. He turned it into a des-res when he built the 'great hall' and the folly. The place was almost derelict for some years, but about ten years ago, it was completely renovated and it is now offices. When an old wash-house was demolished and rebuilt, the remains of a woman and child were found. Forensics suggested that they had been there for about 100-150 years. Was this the origin of 'the grey lady' said to haunt the top floor?

About seven years ago, I was looking after my daughter's cat. I was divorced and living alone, so I did not mind. On several occasions I saw what I thought was the cat and it turned out that the cat was asleep elsewhere. On at least two of the occasions it was on the stairs. Once it was just a dark shape which in an instant reached the top, jumped up, arched its back and ran down again. As it was out of the corner of my eye, I put it down to imagination. My son also saw it once. He was sitting on the sofa and could swear he saw it by the front door. The snag was, the cat was lying next to him asleep on the settee.

As I said, I put it down to imagination until one day when I was sitting on the same settee as my son. It was about 13.00 and my son had come in for dinner from college. I was sitting opposite him by the front door, and I asked him if he had seen the cat. Just as I said that, I distinctly saw a little black leg with distinctive white paw protrude from behind the sofa and reach out to the crack in the door leading to the next room. 'Oh!' I said, 'She's behind you'. As I said that, I noticed a light that seemed brighter than usual shining through the wider-then-normal space under the door (thanks to my expert DIY). In the light, I saw a shadow moving about. With that my heart started thumping. I opened the door and looked down at the cat innocently sitting there. No other cat or any other animal could have got into the house as I NEVER leave windows or outer doors open.

My ex-wife passed away on a Saturday in November 2000 and

Church of St Nicholas and the ancient school house in Kings Norton, from a drawing by Oliver Baker, published in Brassington's 'Historic Worcester-shire', pub-lished 1894.

during the following sad week I had a number of weird experiences. On the night of the following Tuesday, I was working night shift as a security guard in the gatehouse of a nearby factory when the first odd thing happened. The factory makes car parts and had about 200 employees at that time. It is a modern building in two sections. The front part was two-storey but only the upper floor was used as offices during the daytime. The lower manufacturing section had fallen into disuse well before I arrived.

At about 6.00 pm the only person in the office block was the lone cleaner, a woman of about thirty. She came running down to me in a state of terror. She told me that while working in the main office she saw the handle of the door to the disused section turn several times, so she came directly to me. I immediately went to investigate and found the doors secure. Nobody could possibly get in without permission.

That wasn't the only incident that night. Later, at about 3.40am, I was in the disused section checking around but nothing happened until I left the building. In the twenty or so yards between the office door and the gatehouse is a bit of a car park and an external wall about eight feet high and a corner to a utility building. When I walked past I heard a strange voice which I could only describe at the time as a manic rap singer. It was a dark corner, but just light enough to see if there was someone there. As there are four inch gaps in the wall at intervals, I thought it was somebody on the other side and the sound was coming through the gap. The odd thing about the voice is that it seemed to be talking to someone else who answered briefly. It seemed to have an Afro-Caribbean accent and I would describe it now as 'speaking in tongues'. As I approached the corner, I said 'Hello' . At this the voices stopped. I immediately ran round into the street but it was deserted. If there was anyone, they must have done the four minute mile. But they had no reason to run anyhow. People walking past sound different. The voices sounded as if they were coming from the corner.

In the week following the death of my ex-wife, I was in the bathroom and I could swear I saw the cat crawl under the bath. Three times I told the cat to come out. When I looked round, there was the cat the other end of the house by the front door, looking at me perplexed. As the cat is still alive and kicking, I can't call it a ghost. I have never had the experience since.

On the following Saturday, the fourth and last incident occurred. I was going to my late ex- wife's stepbrother's house. My son, daughter and her widower were there. I rang the doorbell and her sister in law, along with my son and my ex's husband came to the door. When she saw me she jumped back nearly knocking my son and stepfather over. When I asked what was wrong, they replied that the bell had rung several times but when they went to answer it, nobody was there.

LEDBURY – The Lone Rider

Ledbury is actually just inside Herefordshire, and near the junction of two other counties, Worcestershire and Gloucestershire. Most of the town was built between 1570 and 1630 when it was an important cloth-making and tanning centre. St Michael's Church in Ledbury was built by the Normans almost nine hundred years ago to replace an even older building. It is unusual in that it has a detached bell tower. The church door is riddled with bullet holes from a civil war skirmish.

In the time of the civil war, Ledbury was a large open village where two main roads intersected, one from Gloucester to Hereford and the other from Worcester to Ross. It was therefore in an important position. In 1645, Ledbury was occupied by the Parliamentarians under Colonel Massey and security was poor. Prince Rupert, who was at Hereford, was determined to dislodge them. Under cover of darkness he marched his army the 16 miles from Hereford to Ledbury for a surprise attack. Quietly, he ordered some of his men round to the Gloucester and Ross side of the village, where they were to wait. Then, with the rest of his men, he burst into the town on the Hereford side. The Parliamentarians fell back to the waiting troops on the Gloucester side. Many of the Parliamentarians tried to escape and were chased for many miles before they were cornered and slaughtered. Prince Rupert sought Colonel Massey for a personal fight and managed to shoot his horse from under him.

The Royalists claimed that 120 Parliamentarians had been killed, the Parliamentarians said that it was only six or seven. The Royalists claimed to have 400 prisoners, the Parliamentarians said that it was only 120. However, a tragic note is that the Parliamentarians claimed that many of the prisoners were not soldiers, but the ordinary villagers caught up in the fighting. On display inside the church is a sword from that very battle.

Perhaps the skirmish has also left some impressions on time!

Freddie Buck is one of the best-known men in Worcestershire. He was secretary to the National Farmers Union for nearly 38 years, starting in 1949. The National Farmers Union is a powerful group, It was founded by nine

Lincolnshire farmers in1904 as the Lincolnshire Farmers Union and grew rapidly to include farmers across the British Isles. It has influenced farming policy every since.

Freddie says he is an arch sceptic, he doesn't believe in the supernatural, the occult or anything like that. However, between 9.00 and 9.30 on New Year's Eve 2002 he had an inexplicable experience:

I had been to Hereford to visit a relative and was coming back along the road from Hereford to Ledbury (A438). My former wife was in the car with me. I was 200 yards from the junction of the Ledbury road and the B4214 Bishops Frome road (another road goes off in the direction of Worcester), when the headlights of the car picked up an apparition of a man on horseback.

We just saw him as a silhouette. He was riding a large horse and I would think dressed in the fashion of 200 years ago. He was wearing a classic hat with a fairly flat pyramid on top and a wide brim, and a full-length coat was draping down. There was no up and down movement, he was gliding, and he went straight across the road in front of us. It was very real.

We both exclaimed, 'Look at that!'.

MARTIN HUSSINGTREE – Smashes and Crashes

Halfway between the Droitwich and Worcester suburbs are the rural villages of Fernhill Heath and Martin Hussingtree. The latter was originally two separate villages, Martin and Hussingtree, both were given to Pershore Abbey by a Saxon king. In the 1500s the Lord of the Manor was so poverty-stricken that the family, the Rudings, had 'scarce cotes to clothe them'.

The area is rich in history. Here the A38 tends to follow the line of the old Roman Road. To the south is Hindlip House, owned by the Habington family, who were staunch Roman Catholics and plotted against the Church of England monarchy. In 1582 they were involved in a plot to set Mary Queen of Scots on the throne and, as a result, Edward Habington lost his head. After the gunpowder plot of 1605 the house was surrounded and two priests were starved out of a priest hole, to be hung, drawn and quartered. Later, the builder of the priest holes was also caught here and tortured to death.

Our intrepid ghost-hunter, Mr Thomas, has been researching the area:

To the north of Fernhill Heath is Martin Hussingtree, where there is a very sharp bend in the road, near to Hindlip Hall, where the police headquarters is based. Near to the common lands, where gypsies put their horses and caravans on the Worcester and Droitwich road, there have been many serious accidents in the past years. An acquaintance of mine, Pam, said to me that when she moved to Fernhill Heath in the 1970s, some of her neighbours and friends told her about a haunted stage-coach that goes around the bend and cars have to swerve out of the way so as not to crash into it. The old Roman road goes straight on from the bend at that spot.

John Rogers O'Shea from Droitwich told me that near Copcut, past the Copcut Elm inn, at the bottom of the hill, near to a fruit and vegetable shop, was a bend where there were many car crashes in the 1950s. John told me that his father was a Police Sergeant in the Worcester and Droitwich police force during the 1950s and that all the people in the accidents reported that they had seen a ghostly lady riding a white horse in front of them on the road. It scared them out of their skins and caused them to crash their cars.

In the 1960s a new bypass was built on the A38 at that spot.

The Copcut Elm was built as a coaching inn by John Amphlett in 1806. During the 1990s it was taken over by the MAD O'Rourke chain to become 'Trotter Hall'. During this period it became one of the most haunted inns in Worcestershire. Phantom guests appeared and disappeared. Large utensils disappeared. Coins flew out of the cigarette machine. The head cook walked into the kitchen and all the gas cookers went 'pow' and lit themselves. The inn has now changed hands and has reverted to the original name of 'Copcut Elm'.

Hindlip Hall in 1776, near Martin Hussingree.
It has been rebuilt and is now used as the
West Mercia Constabulary Headquarters.

POWICK – 'They that shall not grow old'

The River Severn and River Teme meet near Powick, which gives it great importance. There are now two bridges, the old one, dating from the 1400s, and a newer one built in 1837.

The first, and part of the last, battle of the Civil War took place here. The first was little more than a skirmish. It took place on a hot day in the summer of 1642. A small contingent of mounted Parliamentarians trotted happily across the bridge over the Teme. The lane leading from the bridge was narrow with high hedges each side. As the Parliamentarians emerged into an open field, they saw, to their astonishment, a detachment of Royalists resting and enjoying the sunshine. Among the Royalists were Princes Rupert and Maurice, they immediately leaped on to their horses and charged into the enemy. The Parliamentarians were too surprised to fight. They tried to turn and escape, but the lane was too narrow. There was utter confusion. Some were trampled by their horses, others fell into the river. The fighting was sharp. Some historians reckon that 50 of the Parliamentarians were killed, wounded or drowned, and every Royalist officer except Prince Rupert was wounded in some way. Those Parliamentarians who were able fled to Upton, then on to Pershore. The lane was christened 'cut-throat lane', now renamed Swinton Lane.

The old bridge at Powick.

*Holes made by musket
shot in the outer wall
of the tower of Powick
church*

The role of Powick in the final battle has been outlined in the first chapter of this book. In a field known as 'the Ham' near the bridge are two depressions in the ground, said to be two pits into which the bodies were thrown.

All kinds of strange tales come from Powick. One of the residents said that every house in Powick is haunted and even the butcher's had an invisible something that nudged people waiting in the queue. The latest is from a musician, Mr Raymond:

When I lived in Worcester I had an important appointment in Warndon for four o'clock but, as I was cycling through Powick, the pedal fell off my bicycle. I started walking back home, pushing the bike and carrying the pedal. Then all of a sudden, a nut appeared on the road right in front of my eyes, I watched it appear. It was brass and really shining as if it had just been made. Not only was it the right thread but it had to fit inside a barrel and it was the right size for the barrel. I had a pair of long-nosed pliers on me for my job in Warndon so I screwed the pedal back on the bike and tightened it as much as I could with the pliers. I got to my destination just on time.

I was three houses away from my home when the nut came off the bike and the pedal fell off again. The nut bounced on the road and disappeared. I never found it again.

ROWNEY GREEN – Pestilence Lane

Although the small village of Rowney Green is near the A42, it still manages to keep its rural identity. Industries here are few, but, until recently, the BCIRA (British Cast Iron Research Association) was one of them. It was founded in 1924 but has now merged with SCRATA (Steel Castings and Research Association) to form the CTI (Castings Technology International).

The fellow who told the next story is about seventeen stone with muscles and tattoes all over his body and the thought of him having a weep stretches the imagination:

When I was a kid I used to work at BCIRA, at Bordesley Hall, Rowney Green, up the Holloway.

One dark night, I was with a young lady in a mini in a little lane nearby. The car was stationary and I won't go into details about what we were doing. Suddenly, a little light appeared round the bend so we both stopped and looked. First of all we thought it was a pushbike headlamp but as it came nearer it appeared to be somebody with a lantern. Whoever was carrying the lantern was swinging it so that as it went along it wrote a series of ellipses.

It came nearer and nearer and when I saw it close by I thought I was going to cry. For the figure was ten feet tall and the lantern swung high over the roof of the mini. Then it disappeared, the banks were really steep and there was nowhere it could have gone.

I found an old farmyard where I could turn round and drove away. A few days later I was telling an old guy about it and he said, 'Well, you know where you were parked, don't you?' I said, 'No', and he answered, 'In Pestilence Lane'.

If anyone knows which 'pestilence' this refers to, we would be glad to hear it. All down the centuries there have been plagues and epidemics of diseases unheard of today - tuberculosis, scarlet fever, typhoid, smallpox, cholera and so on. Rowney Green is near Alcester, and, as we have said, in 1236 they were hit by a terrible outbreak of the plague, killing the Bishop of Worcester, William de Blois, who was staying there. The site of the plague pit, where the bodies were buried, is not known. Bubonic plague occurred every generation for three centuries.

SALFORD PRIORS AND ABBOTS SALFORD
Salford Hall and the Queen's Head (Iron Cross)

On the Worcestershire/Warwickshire border are two villages a mile apart, Salford Priors and Abbots Salford, both are situated on the road between Evesham and Stratford-on-Avon. Historians state that this was originally a saltway from Droitwich so that Salford Priors was originally named Salteford Major, and Abbots Salford was Salteford Minor, but St Mary's Priory at Kenilworth was given the first village and the Abbots of Evesham the second so the names were changed respectively.

Salford Hall at Abbots Salford, now a hotel, is a grand medieval house of great beauty which has long had the reputation of being haunted. The date over the door says 1602 but it was built before then, in the 1400s, for the Abbots of Evesham. A ghostly priest is so well known that the hotel often holds Murder and Mystery evenings, hoping that he will put in an appearance.

The Salford Hotel story of two little American girls, Wyom and Evra, has not been published in a book for fifteen years (to our knowledge), so we are repeating it below:

From 1807 to 1838 the Hall was occupied by a community of Benedictine

nuns who had been forced to leave Cambrai because of the French Revolution. To make ends meet, they converted the Hall into a girl's boarding school.

One morning in 1815, a coach and horses raced up to the main doors at great speed. A man and two little girls got out, the man ushered them quickly into the office of the Abbess and laid a large sum of money on her desk. He asked her to look after the two little girls until they were eighteen, then place a certain advertisement in 'The Times'.

The two little girls were very happy at the school. The money ran out but the nuns continued to look after them. When Wyom reached eighteen, the advertisement was placed in 'The Times' as requested, and a letter arrived telling Wyom to go to a certain address. Off she went and nothing was heard for some months, which worried the Abbess as Evra and Wyom were very close and Wyom was not the sort of girl to neglect her letter-writing. Even more worrying, Evra began walking in her sleep. The nuns tried to follow her to see where she went but she seemed to disappear into thin air. She told the nuns that she could see Wyom being held prisoner.

The Mother Superior made enquiries and discovered that the address to which Wyom was sent did not exist. She notified the police and a general alert was raised.

In far distant Buckingham a certain Doctor Lapel was called to attend to a young girl under mysterious circumstances. He notified the police and Wyom was found. Evidently, her guardian's son had kidnapped her and was trying to get his hands on her inheritance by forcing her to sign certain documents. When the police found him, he was in a state of 'abject terror' and said that every time he began to bully Wyom, the ghost of a young girl appeared and would not leave him alone.

Salford Hall Hotel, Abbots Salford

Wyom recovered from her ordeal and married the young doctor who had rescued her. Eleven years later a little Wyom Evra Hendon started school at Salford Hall.

A mile down the road towards Evesham, at the Iron Cross in Salford Priors, is The Queen's Head which threatened to rival Salford Hall in its hauntings.

In 2006 Andrew was at the Vauxhall in Evesham but two years previously, in 2004, he had been keeping on eye on the Queens Head for the owners:

It wasn't my pub, I was just looking after it for three months. A manager was living there, there wasn't any need for him to live in but he and his daughter were staying there from choice.

The boiler wasn't working and the pub was cold. I said to them, 'You can't stay here without any heating' and they said, 'Oh, that's alright, we've moved into one of the smaller rooms upstairs, it's in the middle of two other rooms so it's quite warm'.

Anyway, I called the engineer in and he said the boiler had to be replaced. He left it in pieces in the kitchen. A few days later I went over to make sure that the boiler had been repaired. It hadn't, it was still in pieces in the kitchen. The manager and his daughter insisted that they wanted to stay on. They said that the middle bedroom was nice and warm and took me upstairs to show me the room.

As they opened the door, the blast of heat hit me, it was like walking into an oven. I touched the radiator and it wasn't just warm, it was red hot. You couldn't put your hand on it. Yet the boiler was in pieces and the rooms each side were icy cold. I couldn't understand it.

It was an eerie experience. There were loads of stories about that place. It broadened my outlook.

The pub has been burned down a couple of times and the pub had a blackened-out look.

Unfortunately, the present licensee, Deborah, says that she has been the licensee for two years and nothing strange has happened since she has been there. The publishers would love to hear any unusual tales from the past. Our address is in the front of the book.

SEDGEBERROW – The Living Ghost

The straggling little village of Sedgeberrow is sandwiched between the Vale of Evesham and the Cotswold Hills. There has been a thriving community here for at least 700 years as the church, St Mary's, was consecrated in 1331.

George Gregg, MSc, MA, CertEd, the Research Officer for Parasearch, was fortunate to spend his childhood years there. He tells the next two

Sedgeberrow.

stories and offers a variety of explanations:

When I was 13 years of age and lived with my Parents in Churchill Road, Sedgeberrow, I had an interesting experience. I had not long got home from school and I was watching children's TV (Blue Peter, I think) when my father came into the living room. His normal behaviour, as a Linesman's Mate (he worked for the MEB) was to cycle over to Hinton-on-the-Green, about two miles away, in the morning and do the return trip at night getting home about 5.00 pm (with a few minor variations, each day).

I had the chair facing the TV, he touched me on my left shoulder and said something like '....alright Son?'. I explained that I was watching something but would be with him in about five minutes. I looked over my right shoulder and he was combing his hair in the mirror.

However when the TV programme finished I went down the back garden to look for him. I had something to tell him (but it's so long ago now I forget what it was about). There was no sign of him. I asked my mother who was preparing the main evening meal where my dad had gone. She had no idea and was adamant that he had not come home yet.

As she was completely deaf, (due to a childhood illness) I assumed he had come into the house without her hearing and that he was there, somewhere, although I must admit it was hard to imagine him arriving home without speaking to my mother. A search of the house and garden left me completely bewildered.

There was no doubt in my mind that he had been there. He had spoken to me, he had touched me and I had seen him. He had been there, that was all there was to it. So why was he playing a trick on my mother and myself?

About fifteen to twenty minutes later whilst I was standing at the front gate puzzling about this experience I saw my dad push biking along Churchill Road on his way home. After quizzing him intensely he convinced me that this was the first time he had been home, at least physically anyway. There had been no crisis and my father had not experienced a shock, an accident or unconsciousness during the time of my experience. This phenomenon has left a marked impact on me for the rest of my life. I'm in my fifties now and still puzzle about what happened.

Paranormal Explanation: There are other examples of ghosts of the living and this may be an example of out of body experience (OBE) or Extra Sensory Perception (ESP). Psychical researchers have noticed that when people observe an apparition they are often in an altered state of consciousness. If both my father, who was carrying out a relatively mindless activity of cycling and I had done the same, it could be that our minds reached out and contacted each other.

Psychological Explanation: As I was watching TV I was in an altered state of consciousness (ASC) and therefore on the borderlands between waking and sleeping and possibly experienced a lucid dream.

SPETCHLEY, WHITE LADIES AND PEOPLETON

The Bloody Paintings

Spetchley Hall is less than a mile from Nunnery Wood. In the time of the Civil War it was owned by Sir Robert Berkeley, a Royalist. The building was burned down, not by the Parliamentarian troops but by Presbyterian members of the Royalist army! Sir Robert made the stables habitable and lived there until he died.

Not far away is a large Elizabethan manor house. A local farmer told us:

I was in Birmingham market where I bumped into an old friend of mine, a tall man with ginger hair. He asked me, 'How long have you been living there?'. I asked him how he knew where I lived. He answered, 'I saw you cutting the lawn. How do you find it?'. 'Alright'

Worcestershire, the Haunted County

Spetchley Park in Victorian times.

I said. We chatted on for a bit and I asked him, 'Why are you so interested in my place?'. He said, 'We lived just up the road from you, at the top of the hill'. I asked, 'How long did you live there?'. He said, 'Too long'. 'What do you mean, too long?'. He told me, 'It was a b...terrible place. Nobody could stay there. It was haunted'.

He said, 'When we were living there the ceilings of the top floor rooms in the house had paintings on them. We had somebody to look at them and sent scrapings away and they were done with blood. Week in and week out we used to have people walking through the walls and there was banging and clashing all night long. We couldn't get a wink of sleep. We had only been there two or three weeks and we put it on the market again and it took us eight or ten years to sell it. We heard that somebody had been murdered in that house'.

Although it may sound macabre, it is not all that unusual to find paintings done with blood. In medieval times, ox blood was often used and sometimes the entire outside of the house was painted with it, giving an attractive dark red appearance. However, it is unusual to have people walking out of your walls and if the friend who lived in the house would like to get in touch with Hunt End Books, we would love him to tell his story – anonymously of course.

White Ladies and Dark Deeds

To the east of Spetchley is White Ladies, which takes its name from the fact that, until Henry VIII appropriated all church property, it was owned by the Nunnery of Whitstones in Worcester.

White Ladies has a traditional Civil War ghost. In his book 'The Folklore of Worcestershire', Roy Palmer states that a short distance from the Symond's mansion at White Ladies, was Lovers' Lane, where a Muriel Symonds kept a secret rendezvous with her Royalist lover. Unfortunately, he was killed at the Battle of Naseby in 1645. Muriel began walking in her sleep and talking to him as if he were alive. After her death it was said that her ghost walked the lane in white satin every year on June 15th, the eve of the Battle of Naseby.

At the time of the Civil War, Aston Court was known as Stone Court and was occupied by the Goods family. They were Royalists and Stone Court was plundered by the Parliamentarians. The 'Victoria County History' states:

> The Puritan commander, noticing a pretty Miss Good, became very rude in his attentions, and to save herself from outrage she fled into a neighbouring wood where she climbed into a tree and shrouded herself among the thick foliage and thus escaped further notice. The tree was long honoured in the family, but yielding to time and age like all sublunary things, only its stump was last left in the wood.

The White Lady of White Ladies

In the parish of White Ladies is the straggling village of Peopleton. Copyright forbids us from quoting the section on Peopleton in the 'Worcestershire Village Book', but it portrays a lively society in a village without street lights, doctor, police station and with minimal bus services. The number of half-timbered buildings and the early medieval parts of St Nicholas suggest an ancient settlement and, indeed, Peopleton is mentioned in King Edgar's charters of 792.

One of its ex-residents is Mick Knott, a sensible and intelligent man. He was a bomber pilot during World War II.

> It sounds so daft. It seems years ago now but it must have been in the late 1960s that this happened. I had a got a fruit farm near Peopleton, between Pershore and Worcester, at a place called Walsgrove. From Spetchley Cross Roads, you took the road to Pershore and our farm was exactly one mile to where you turned in at the farm gate.
>
> I went up to Stafford to a British Legion meeting and when I came back late at night I was in the car on my own. I passed through Spetchley and turned along the road to Pershore. Three quarters of the way to my farm you went up a bit of a rise and when you reached the top of the hill there was a very old black and white house, Low Hill, among dark trees.
>
> It was latish and I was really shifting, I was doing about 80 and as I went over the top a woman ran out of a gateway with her arms above her head. She was dressed in a long - well - the type of clothes like you see in the Watteau paintings. I went straight through her! I was so shocked I swerved and I just tipped the bank with my wheels. She had come through a gate and inside this gate was an old pond and a

... as I went over the top a woman ran out of a gateway with her arms above her head. She was dressed in a long - well - the type of clothes like you see in the Watteau paintings. I went straight through her!

pear tree, leaning almost parallel to the ground.

When I got home my wife said, 'What's the matter with you, you look as if you have seen a ghost!' I said, 'I b...well have! I went straight through her, just like that!'. After that I didn't think about it much, we talked about it sometimes and that was all.

Across the road and a little way down were some cottages. The woman was running out of the gateway of Low Hill house into these cottages opposite. Some years afterwards I noticed that the cottages were gone. When I mentioned this to my wife she said that they had been gone for some time.

If you came out of our gate and turned left, about thirty or forty yards further on was the road that went to White Ladies Aston. I have been told that the field in the corner was known as Bishop Lloyd's charity and it was taken from a murderer before he was hanged and given over to the Bishop.

The pond has been filled in, the pear tree has gone and so perhaps the frightened lady has retired to rest.

Peopleton is only approximately five miles from the site of the Battle of Worcester and the whole area suffered badly. The Spetchley estate was burned to the ground, as previously mentioned. A mile to the north of Peopleton is Upton Snodsbury. In his excellent booklet, 'A Short History of Upton Snodsbury', Mr Eagle points out that although the village existed for about a thousand years before the Civil War, the only complete building left today which pre-dates the battle is the Church. He suspects that Upton Snodsbury suffered the same fate as Spetchley. What disaster occurred at nearby Peopleton to send a terrified lady running into the road, so distraught that she created an impression on time?

STUDLEY – Prayers and Miracles

Just over the border, in Warwickshire, is one of the largest villages in England – Studley. The Roman Icknield Street runs through it and in early medieval times it had a castle and a priory. The latter was well-known for its naughty monks. In 1384 the Prior of Worcester came to admonish the monks for their lax behaviour and was met with bows and arrows. In the reign of Henry VI the Prior kept an unofficial wife in Skilts, the priory grange.

The village pub, the Barley Mow, was a favourite lodging place of John Wesley, a founder of the Wesleyan Methodist Church.

In the village is an odd combination, a modern house with an ancient shed. There's a story attached:

We had a fairly new house on the main road and at the bottom of the garden was an old garden shed – like a potting shed.

Things in the house used to get moved around, you would put something down in one place and it would turn up in another. I remember one day a huge rush of wind swept through the house and slammed a door shut, yet it was a still day with no wind and there was no through draught.

My husband went to work in Manchester and I tried to sell the house so that I could join him but it was on the market for a year and nobody bought it.

Then one of our friends came to visit, and one of the wives said, 'Do you mind if I say a prayer here?'. This house makes me feel ill at ease, I feel that there's an evil presence here. It's manifested in the potting shed, something terrible has happened in there.

Well, I don't believe in that sort of thing but I said I didn't mind and the prayer was said. To my astonishment, the house sold within the next two weeks. Someone came to look at the house who had been a few months previously, and she said, 'Have you redecorated? The house is so much brighter than when we last saw it'.

STOKE PRIOR – What the Milkman Saw

Stoke Prior was once well-known for its salt, now it has achieved fame as the home of Avoncroft, highly recommended as a family day out. All kinds of buildings have been renovated from medieval houses to a Victorian prison, and they also include a windmill, an ice house and the Gueston Hall roof from Worcester Cathedral. While you are there, ask the staff about their ghosts. There were so many strange happenings that a paranormal team was called in to investigate.

The wealth of history at Avoncroft tends to overshadow Stoke Prior's Norman church, dedicated to St Michael and much of it built around 1200. Strange to say, ghosts in churchyards are very rare but one was seen approaching St Michael's churchyard in the early morning.

We have Mr Thomas to thank for this story:

My local milkman, Nigel, said to me that he had a ghostly experience early one morning. Driving his milk van along the Bromsgrove to Hanbury Road near Stoke Prior, he was going past the old Ewe and Lamb pub, down the hill and around the bend towards Stoke Prior church, when he saw a ghostly vision and a mist walking right in front of the van. He had to swerve around it so to get out of its way and not to hit it. The ghostly mist walked across the road towards the old churchyard. He was very startled and shook up.

TARDEBIGGE – 'Nature's soft nurse'

A slip road off the Bromsgrove Highway from Bromsgrove to Redditch takes you to Tardebigge. The spire of St Bartholemew tops a hill and can be seen for miles around, particularly when illuminated at night. The fifth Lord Windsor is buried here, and the Sixth Earl of Plymouth. Until the 19th century the boundary of Worcestershire and Warwickshire ran through the church. Thomas Habington was a Roman Catholic and, in the reigns of Queen Elizabeth and King James, implicated in various plots against the throne. There's a tradition that, as a punishment, he was not allowed to go outside Worcestershire. He spent his days researching the history of the county but when it came to Tardebigge, he had to stand in the main body of the church and peer into the chancel as this was in Warwickshire!

Beside the church, a steep hill drops down to the Worcester to Birmingham canal and the country's longest flight of narrow locks. A stone's throw from the Church is the Hewell Grange estate, once a grange for Bordesley Abbey, then the seat of the Earls of Plymouth. It has come down in the world and is now a Remand Home with Blakenhurst and Brockenhurst prisons in the grounds.

The hotel, 'The Tardebigge' opposite Hewell Grange is no less interesting. It was built by the Earl of Plymouth as a community centre for the villagers in 1911, but the villagers have not been able to enjoy their gift for many years. In the first world war it was used as a hospital and then two Earls of Plymouth died in rapid succession. Various estates had to be sold off to offset the heavy death duties. It was sold to Ansells Brewery in 1946.

Two pint tankards shatter for no reason, staff hear their name called and feel taps on the shoulder, phantom laughter is heard and cleaning ladies

The Tardebigge, said to be haunted by a nurse.

159

leave suddenly. In the early 1990s paranormal incidents became such a nuisance that a paranormal expert, Anne Jones was called in to investigate. She felt that the hotel was haunted by Emily, a nurse from the First World War, and she identified Emily from an old photograph.

Victoria works as a waitress at the Tardebigge.

The old nurse has often been seen at Table 28 and it's very cold in that corner. I was waiting for the pub to open one morning and when I got in I saw thick smoke suddenly appeared at that one table. When I've been working in the bar, someone keeps flicking my ear but when I turn round, no-one is there.

Victoria's mother says that she had seen the nurse.

Four of us had gone for a meal and were in the sitting room area when suddenly she was there in a long dark dress. I was the only one that saw her.'

WARNDON - The Old Man and the Child

The M5 reached Warndon in the 1950s and what was once a tiny village a mile east of Worcester, is now a sprawling housing estate. This is not all bad news, for the Norman church of St Nicholas, which was so ruinous that snow had to be swept off the altar before a Christmas service, has been completely renovated. The 16th century black and white tower is now in pristine condition and the stained glass in the east window portraying a Virgin and dating back to the 1300s, has been restored.

Warndon is mentioned in the Domesday Survey of 1086. Both the grey friars and the black friars held land here which they lost to Henry VIII in about 1539 when the king dissolved the monasteries.

A young couple moved into a newly built house in Warndon, Worcester, several years ago. The wife says:

'The last thing we expected was for it to be haunted, as it was built on farmland. For the first two months our youngest daughter, at that time only 3 years old, was woken regularly at night complaining she could see an old man staring at her in her bedroom by the window. It got so bad that we were all suffering illnesses through lack of sleep!

My husband regularly saw apparitions of a little girl dressed in a white nightgown, who took great delight in looking at our Halloween masks and making the sensor light come on in the back garden. That same spot in the garden where my husband saw the little girl was popular with the local cats. I counted three all lying together in the same spot one day - are they attracted by child ghosts?

Around the same time, my husband had a dream that an old man and a little girl were starving to death in an old cottage on the same site but their manner of dress suggested that it happened many years ago.

Another time we got up the next morning to find a vase of flowers had moved some considerable distance to the middle of the living room floor. Other times we would wake and see the child's outline between us in bed before it shot out of the window! Electricity was a major problem and contractors were called out regularly. The heating would come on all by itself when completely turned off. We got it checked by an electrician who said that he couldn't think why that would happen as it was in perfect working order.

We also discovered that the lane near the estate was called the 'Haunted Lane' which may have taken injured Civil War soldiers up to the Grange (an old manor pulled down and replaced by a pub on the Lippards).

We found out subsequently that there had been a plague in the 14th Century which had wiped out most of the old village, there was also a famine; the Church of St Nicholas is not surrounded by a village as such - indicative of villagers fleeing. I also found out afterwards that an archaeological dig produced medieval items very near our new house suggesting buildings from that period. After contacting the local council, I found out that the ditch surrounding part of the site of our house may have been Roman in origin.

Another interesting point is that after we had told a neighbour of our disturbances they said that a couple of other families on the estate

A painting of St Nicholas, Warndon, in 1810.

were also being haunted by an old man and a little girl dressed in white.

Warndon is less than five miles from the centre of Worcester and injured soldiers may very well have been taken to the old manor house. With reference to the plague, as we have said elsewhere, there were outbreaks of bubonic plague for three successive centuries, but the worst one came in 1348/9. Fields were deserted, houses stood empty and mills were idle and unrepaired. It is unlikely that any village in Worcestershire would have escaped. However, the Black Death is not always the reason for a deserted village, for example, the villagers could simply have spotted better soil elsewhere.

WYCHBOLD – The Eerie Airship

The route of the old Roman road, Icknield Street, has been fairly well preserved between Bromsgrove and Droitwich by the B4091 and A38. About two miles from Droitwich is Wychbold, mentioned in the Domesday Survey. Two of its early owners met with violent deaths. In the 11th century it belonged to the Prior of Worcester but the wicked Edwin 'wrested it from them!'. Edwin was eventually put to death by the King of the Britons. Then in 1304, it belonged to Hugh Mortimer who died after being poisoned by his wife, Maude.

Wychbold is now well-known for several reasons. The original Domesday manor has been replaced by the 700 feet high masts of the BBC station. They were completed in 1934 and programmes were actually broadcast from here. Opposite the masts is the enormous Webb's garden centre, nearby is junction 5 of the M5 and two miles nearer to Droitwich is the magnificent 1870s Chateau Impney. It is advisable to drive carefully along here for, on dark and stormy nights, a tall, thin phantom hitch-hiker in a dark floor-length coat has been seen several times.

Most locals know that the Chateau was built by the Salt King, John Corbett. John was an ordinary working man but he was left a small sum of money with which he bought up old salt mines at Stoke Prior and, in 1828, using the latest industrial methods, revived both the salt mines and Stoke Prior. He then turned his attention to run-down Droitwich and reversed its fortunes by making it into a spa town.

However, not many know that he paid for new hospitals in Bromsgrove and Stourbridge, he contributed heavily to Birmingham University and in 1888/9, he also built Wychbold Church. Astwood Lane is near the Church and in the 1950s Joan used to live in an old cottage there:

It was one of four built in a square. Before then it had been a Dame

School and before that a chapel. I have tried to find out how old it was without success, but I would think it would go back to the late 1700s. The cottages were knocked down in the 1960s and two modern semi-detached houses built on the site.

When I was about 14 my cousin came to stay. One bright, sunny day, we had been down to the village on an errand for my mother and we were walking as if we were going from the village looking towards the church and the cottage. Suddenly, from nowhere, this huge cigar-shaped airship appeared. You know in the airship that blew up, there was a kind of basket underneath for passengers, but in this one there was nothing underneath, and no propellors. It was just one big balloon. As to the size of it - it was absolutely huge. It dwarfed the cottages where we lived. It appeared from

An early airship, this model had no visible basket underneath.

nowhere and hovered. My cousin and I just looked at it. We were not frightened - more mesmirised. Then it just went. It didn't fade, it shot off as if it was catapulted backwards. It made no sound.

We were quite shocked. We went running home to mother. She had been in the garden, hanging the washing out but she hadn't seen it.

My cousin died when she was quite young but before then, every time we met or we spoke on the phone we said, 'Do you remember ...'.

SECRET VENUES

ntil the end of the 18th century lunatics in institutions were often cruelly treated. Gradually, however, modern methods prevailed and patients in mental hospitals are usually today nursed with care and kindness. However, mental disorders are still at the cutting edge of medicine, and sometimes a cure is attempted which causes suffering to the patient. In the early 1900s, Pavlov won a Nobel Prize for his work on conditioned reflexes. One of his theories was that electric shocks could cure some kinds of mental diseases. Although the use of Electro-convulsive therapy (ECT) is now declining, for many years electric shocks were given to people with severe depression, manic depression or schizophrenia who had not responded to treatment.

The patient is anaethetised and given an injection of muscle relaxant, which depresses the breathing. Oxygen is given until the patient is able to breathe normally again. Electrodes are placed on the temples and an electrical charge lasting between 1 and 4 seconds is given to the brain, causing an epileptic-like seizure. This usually continues three times a week for about three weeks. The side effects can be severe and can very occasionally cause brain damage.

Over the years the different approaches to mental disorders, such as 'Care in the Community' has seen the closure of a number of mental hospitals in Worcestershire. Some of these have been sold off as building land. Helen* lives in an apartment built on the site of a mental hospital.

A friend of mine worked as the hospital clerk until the hospital closed, and so did her friend, and her friend's mother was a hospital cleaner. They have all said that the apartments are built on the site of the wards of the mental hospital. I went to the history centre and looked at an old map to check. As to what treatment was given on the wards, we can only surmise it could have been electric shock treatment.

All kinds of peculiar things happen here. I sometimes wonder if we have a spirit in the apartment, perhaps someone who was unhappy with the treatment and has come back to haunt the premises. We have many problems with the electricity. I can be sitting here, watching television and suddenly the TV changes channels all by itself. Or, I'm sitting reading and my standard lamp comes on of its own accord. I switch the kettle off at the mains and it switches itself on again. Also, light bulbs keep popping, in the second bedroom, three go in a week. They used to go in the lounge, eight popped in about five months, but that's stopped now. Perhaps the spirit is getting his or her own back!

We have other strange things happening as well. I had only been here three days when I went into my bedroom and found that it was awfully cold, like ice. There was no reason for it, the radiators were on and, as this is an apartment, everything is on the one level. Then I woke up at 2 or 3 o'clock in the morning and smelt bacon and eggs cooking. Who would be cooking bacon and eggs at that time in the morning?

There are other inexplicable smells, sometimes it's perfume. I can smell the perfume at night in my bedroom, it can be quite strong. I remarked about the smell to my cousin. I said I thought it was 'Evening in Paris' as I had an old aunt who used this perfume. I could remember it from a child and I described the shape of the bottle and top. My cousin agreed that it was 'Evening in Paris'. Then I can smell cigarette smoke and I can tell you what that is, it's Cravan A cigarette, it has a strong, distinctive smell. I experience these smells about once a month. Last Thursday I smelt egg and bacon, and last Friday it was perfume.

I sometimes wonder if the spirit walks round in the night and picks things up and hides them. I have more problems with missing items than anything else. It's very annoying. At the moment a big A4 photo of my brother's wedding has gone missing. I know I put it in a certain drawer. A very important letter has gone missing, it came to light once and now it has gone again. I said to my sister, 'The letter was definitely on the shelf in my office but it's gone missing again'. She said, 'You and your spirit'. She doesn't like me to talk about it.

These things turn up in strange places. I took my ring off and put it carefully on the windowsill then when I went to put it back on, it had gone. I hunted high and low for it. A week later, I got my bucket out of the cupboard to do some cleaning and there it was, in the bottom of the bucket under the cleaning cloths. I had a picture of my dog which was very precious. That disappeared and that turned up in the bottom of a cupboard. Sometimes, I have got a pair of earrings out of my jewellery box and then decided not to wear them that day, so I have left them on the dressing table. The next time I look, they are back in the jewellery box.

I don't have fitted furniture in my bedroom so there's a space underneath the wardrobe and things have turned up there. I would never put anything under the wardrobe, it's a very narrow space and difficult to reach into. I have two pairs of favourite shoes and I usually wear either one pair or the other. One pair disappeared and I found them wedged under the wardrobe. I don't put shoes there. I bought a new pair of bathroom scales and they disappeared so I had to buy another set. The first pair turned up under the wardrobe right in the back corner.

There are strange noises in the apartment, I can hear a rustling in the walls and a knocking, but when I go to the door no-one is there. I have a row of ornaments on the window sill and I arrange them so that they are facing towards me. I went out shopping one day and when I came back they were all facing sideways. I have two toy dogs, wire-haired fox terriers, on the back of the settee. They are always placed side by side but some mornings the dogs have been parted overnight.

Sometimes, at night, I walk into my bedroom and it's icy cold. I have had my arm touched so I don't put my arm out of bed now when I'm asleep. I have felt a heavy weight on the duvet as if someone is lying in the centre of my back, I pull the duvet but nothing is there. I was frightened at first but I have got used to it now. Before I go to sleep I say, 'Spirit, don't visit me to tonight, I'll make an appointment to see you'. That makes me feel better.

I have been in this apartment now for three years and I have seen a nurse in uniform about a dozen times. I have got up in the night to go to the toilet, come out of the bedroom and there she is. She's as plain as anything. She's plumpish and in her thirties. The uniform is a whitish grey colour and she's wearing a white bonnet which is gathered in a fan-type pleat at the back of her neck. She's only here for a few seconds, she makes her presence known then she disappears through the bathroom door. I think she likes to have a look and see what's going on. Another time I came out of the bathroom, there's a big mirror in my hall and I could see her shadow behind me in the mirror. This was a military hospital in the war, perhaps she's something to do with that.

Several visitors have remarked that they have a feeling that they are being watched. I leave my bedroom door open as my hallway is dark, and leaving the door open lets light into the hall. My cousin walked past the door and it was open. When she came to leave, her words were, 'When I went to the bathroom that door was open, now it's closed'. I have thick carpet, someone would have to close the door, it would not close on its own. No-one had been near my bedroom door as we were in the lounge talking. My cousin knows about the funny things that happen here.

My neighbours have had problems too. The man who lives in the apartment on the top floor has sat in his lounge and when he has gone into his bedroom to fetch something the closed window was open.

The apartment next to mine is in the next block. A new family moved in, and after they had been there a few weeks I spoke to the

166

chap as I was about to get in my car. He said, 'I hope you don't think I'm mad as we're on the mental hospital site but have you had funny things happen?'. I smiled, and he said, 'You have, haven't you?'. Their television changes channels just like mine and they have been sitting in the lounge when the pictures move. 'Fly around' were the words he used. One night, the husband and wife were fast asleep and the husband moved his leg out of bed in his sleep. He woke up startled. Someone had run his or her hand up the leg that was out of bed. His wife was asleep, she woke up and wondered what was happening. The family have also seen shadows outside the window. Nobody walks at the back of our apartments as it is planted with shrubbery.

My photo is still missing, the letter has turned up again on the desk by my computer. An ornament of a lady on the window sill was turned in the night, she now has her back towards me. I have left her like that as I am fed up of putting her the proper way round.

THE CARE HOME

We have here to thank a lady who has not only given us details of these strange happenings in The Care Home, but has telephoned her friends and persuaded them to talk to us. Unfortunately, she has to remain anonymous.

The Care Home was in Worcestershire in a Victorian red-brick building. It specialised in people with dementia. There is no need to worry whether this is your grandma's Care Home as it has now closed.

The first section is by the former administrator, who gives an overall view of the situation:

So many spooky things happened that the Vicar came in and blessed the premises. It was all taken very seriously.

Evidently things had been happening for a long time, for at least ten years, before I was employed there. At the time we kept it quiet. Many of our patients had Alzheimer's and they wouldn't have been bothered but we didn't want their relatives to think they were being kept in a haunted building.

The vicar was working with the owner in the office when they heard furniture being moved about upstairs. The two of them ran upstairs to have a look but nobody was there, all the residents were in the lounge.

When we had new staff we didn't tell them about the strange goings on, and that was interesting because quite often they'd mention they'd had something peculiar happen. One particular girl who was employed to do the laundry had only been working at the Home a short while, when one day she came running downstairs in tears. She said somebody had just pulled her pony tail whilst she was putting away towels in the upstairs linen cupboard. She'd turned round to find nobody there! When she eventually discovered what was happening she wouldn't go up to the airing cupboard on her own again.

Personally, I had only one minor experience. I was working in the office late one evening on the computer when I felt "someone" apparently put a hand on my knee. I remember brushing it off whilst concentrating on the document I was typing, but didn't think much more about it until the next day when I arrived at work. Everyone was talking about a strange happening the previous night when one of the residents had been waiting for some time by the lift to go upstairs to bed. A carer had asked her why she hadn't got in yet, and the lady replied "I can't - there's a man in a black coat going up and down in the lift!". So when I explained about the hand on my knee incident the staff were goggle-eyed, especially when they heard that I'd walked home alone in the dark after leaving the Home that evening!

A very confused elderly lady often talked about "the man and two children" who used to sit on her bed and talk to her. The carers thought this was just in her imagination, due to her dementia. When this lady died, another resident arrived at the home and took over the same bedroom. The carers were astonished when one morning the new lady started to tell the carer helping her to dress how a man had visited her in the evening and had been sitting on the bed with his two children and had been chatting to her ....

When we lost all the residents the place was empty and as we didn't want squatters, a team of people baby-sat the building. They said that as soon as the tenants left, the whole atmosphere changed and it became nice and warm, a friendly place.

The next section is by a Carer at the Home.

One night I was upstairs putting someone to bed and I was so certain that someone was standing behind me, I rang the bell on the wall for someone to come up and help me.

When residents arrived, we would unpack their belongings then put the empty suitcase in the wardrobe in their room. One night, I went downstairs and there, by the front door, was an empty suitcase belonging to one of the residents. It hadn't been there when I went past previously. All the residents were in bed and although there were two other members of staff, they were in a different part of the house. No-one was coming in or going out, and there was no need for anyone to put an empty suitcase by the door.

Another night, it must have been about nine o'clock, and I was walking towards the office to get the Report Book, we had, of course, to write a full report each night. As I went along the corridor I happened to glance up and someone in white was running across the top of the landing. I couldn't believe what I was seeing. All our residents were bed-ridden. You had to lift them out of bed, get them dressed and sit them in a chair. The thought of one of them running to and fro is laughable. I could see it quite clearly, it was wearing a white floor-length nightgown with a hood, it was plumpish, not very tall and I would say, from its movements, middle-aged. I was so flabbergasted that I just stood there and watched for about five minutes while the figure ran to and fro. Then it just faded away. It was really scary.

After that I got somebody to go with me into the office to get the Report Book. I mentioned the figure in the Report. I said that it had been a dreadful experience.

The following lady was senior carer at the home for many years. She says she coped with the strange events through prayer, she prayed as she went along the corridor and she prayed as she went upstairs.

Sometimes the activity would go on for months. Alarm bells would go off for no reason. Clothes were strewn along the corridor from end to end. We had problems in the laundry late at night, doors would slowly open and close. Staff were called out in the middle of the night because the bathrooms were flooding and no-one seemed able to stop it.

I myself have felt a presence and heard the footsteps going down the corridor. When the presence was about, you had a sense of what it was like. It was male, tall and thin and wearing black and we could only think that it was someone from the Victorian era. He was very heavy-footed. You couldn't mistake his walk.

Most things happened in one particular area. One of the members of my family was covering a night shift, she was carrying the laundry and when she opened the laundry door something smacked her in the face.

We had a male carer working in that area. He went upstairs one morning and felt that there was a presence in the room and that the presence was getting closer and closer. He came downstairs very quickly. Many of our patients were immobile and unable to communicate. In that same room was one such lady and one day her bell went. We all looked at each other. When we went up there we saw that the bed was perfectly and neatly rolled back, her pillow was on the floor and she was lying stretched out on the floor with her head on the pillow, quite happy. There was no way she could have fallen out of bed, everything was arranged so neatly and we would have heard a bump.

There was one such moribund lady in another area. A male carer took her to her bedroom in a wheelchair, then he left her and went to get fresh towels. When he came back she was over the other side of the room. There was no way she could have pulled the brake off.

A member of staff went upstairs to put a resident to bed. There was an old rocking chair in the room and as she opened the door she saw the chair was rocking to and fro, then it tipped forwards as if someone had a hand on each arm and was lifting themselves out of it.

At 10.30 one night everyone was in bed and a carer was hoovering. She heard the heavy footsteps walk across the landing upstairs, then they came down the stairs towards her. She locked herself in the kitchen.

We had one resident who was rather an aggressive lady. When we put her to bed, she demanded that we checked the wardrobe door as there was a man coming out of the wardrobe. Some of the residents were mentally disorientated and we used to hear all kinds of things, but we know this was correct as the man walked through that wall and came out the other side, where he was seen by a male carer!

I had agency girls on my shift. I believe that fear breeds fear, so I made a point of not mentioning the disturbances to any of the agency staff. One of the agency girls came downstairs looking quite ill. She had actually felt a presence and when she tried to move she felt as if she was choking. She was so poorly that I had to send her home. That's when the proprietor decided to send for the Vicar.

The girls would only go upstairs in twos, and when it came towards the evening, the girls would get quite jumpy.

The owner of the property is a qualified psychiatric nurse and was the Proprietor and Manager of the Care Home.

There were a lot of strange goings on every now and again. Everybody heard lots of footsteps going up and down the stairs and across the landing when nobody was about.

I was with some of the other staff when the outside light came on and we all heard a lady in high heels walk up to the front door. We opened the door but no-one was there. We sometimes had agency staff and they didn't know the history of the building and they heard things. We also found that 'it' used to react to us. When we were talking about 'it' we used to hear lots of footsteps and the footsteps used to get quite angry and start stamping.

We had lots of nasty smells like faeces and, being a Care Home we used to go round hunting for the culprit, but there wasn't one and the smell would disappear. They used to come and go for no reason. A strange thing was that they only ever appeared in the staff quarters.

I remember when someone tried to open a wardrobe door but couldn't get the door open properly. It would give for a few inches then close again. It seemed as if someone was holding it from the inside. Then suddenly it opened and we had no more trouble with it.

Silly little things used to disappear, always staff property. Someone would put a handkerchief down and it would be gone. I know once someone lost their spectacles. Even when the place closed down and everything was cleared we didn't find them.

A few of the staff saw a man in a hat. To my knowledge it was seen by two different staff about two years apart. Another lady said she saw a little boy.

On one occasion the night staff called the police because they were so certain they had an intruder. While the police were there, they all heard footsteps coming down the corridor. Everyone went upstairs to have a look round and when they came down the library books had been thrown all over the floor. The policeman said, 'You haven't got an intruder, you have a ghost'. The girls were so frightened that the policeman stayed the night with them.

One of the ladies was in the end stages of her life. She couldn't talk but she could always make it clear what she wanted by just looking at you. The light above her head used to go on and off. Unless I had seen it myself I wouldn't have believed it.

One night I had to stay behind and do the night duty. The two of us on duty heard these noises upstairs, it was as if someone was dragging a desk across the floor. We assumed it was one of the residents as it came from her room so we went upstairs to have a look. We opened the door and the noise stopped. The lady concerned was in a deep sleep and had no awareness of what was going on. We closed the door and the noise started again. The girl with me and I looked at each other. We opened the door again and noise stopped. We closed the door again and the noise started. At that point I realised it was something out of the ordinary, that I hadn't come across before. A cold shiver went down my spine. It was carrying on all night, so we ignored it. Then about four o'clock in the morning the tension seemed to have gone out of the place and I realised that it had stopped.

I knew I was out of my depth and called the vicar in. I thought he would call me stupid or mad but he didn't laugh at me. He came in to bless the building and he did so every year.

When he did the blessing you could feel that the atmosphere lightened, the stress went.

It worked for so long, sometimes as long as 10 months, then things would start again.

There was one occasion in the afternoon, it was a nice sunny day, when the vicar was going round sprinkling holy water, All of a sudden we heard a noise just like someone winding a wet finger round the rim of a wine glass. Everybody heard it.

I can almost pinpoint the time when the last resident left. You could feel all the tension had gone. I said, 'It's gone now'. We closed The Home down on the day that the last person went, and 'the happenings' stopped completely. Until the place was sold one of the staff was there day and night and nothing unusual ever occurred.

Epilogue - The Last of King Charles

On 3rd September 1651, amid the noise and confusion of the great battle, Charles Stuart slipped out of the back door of his quarters in the Corn Market, mounted his horse and was away. Accompanied by a few faithful retainers he seems to have travelled through Ombersley, Hartlebury, Hagley, Pedmore, Stourbridge, Kinver and on to Staffordshire. His horse may have been reshod in Bromsgrove. There was a reward for his capture amounting to millions of pounds in today's money. He was on the run for six weeks, posing as the manservant of Lady Jane Lane. After many exciting adventures he was smuggled on board a boat to take him to France.

Back home, things did not go well for Oliver Cromwell. Parliament was reinstated but after four years members had achieved very little. In fact, they were more concerned with looking after their own interests than governing the country. The real power still lay with Cromwell and the army. On 20th April 1653 Cromwell, despairing at last of Parliament, called in the soldiers. He said, as he dismissed the House, 'You have sat too long here for any good you are doing'. He then ruled as Lord Protector until his death in 1658.

The country, weary of political chaos and narrow legislation, decided to restore the monarchy and Charles was invited back to rule as Charles II on 29th May 1660. And so the monarchy was restored, albeit with an amended constitution. The crown had finally come to Charles. There was really no need for the battle of Worcester.

It is explained in the introduction that some paranormal investigators believe that events involving great emotions leave an impression on time that can be picked up by some individuals in later years. If this is so, then if the Battle of Worcester had not taken place, we would not perhaps have had such stories as Mick Knott's terrified apparition or Freddie Buck's phantom horseman.

BIBLIOGRAPHY

Atkin Malcolm, *The Battle of Worcester 1651*, Harlot Publication 2001.

Brassington W Salt, *Historic Worcestershire*, The Midland Educational, 1894.

Bund Willis J W, *The Civil War in Worcesteshire*, Redwood Burn 1905.

Daniels Janet and Marion Freeman, *Pershore Digest*, Dolwilym Publications 2006.

Davies Pat and Lorna Sage, *Alvechurch Past & Present*, Warwick Printing Company 2002.

Eagle T K, *A Short History of Upton Snodsbury*, privately published 2006.

Foxall Alan, *Old Redditch Pubs*, Token Books 2002.

Fraser Maxwell, *Companion into Worcestershire*, Methuen's Companion Books, 1939.

Harrington Peter, *English Civil War Archaeology*, BT Batsford 2004.

Havins Peter J Neville, *A Portrait of Worcestershire*, Robert Hale 1974.

Holder Len, *River Severn Passenger Steamers 1956-1986*, Len Holder Publications 2006.

Hunt Tristram, *The English Civil War*, Weiderfeld & Nicholson 2002.

Leatherbarrow J S, *Worcestershire*, B T Batsford 1974.

Pevsner Niklaus, *The Buildings of England - Worcestershire*, Penguin Books 1968.

Palmer Roy, *The Folklore of Worcestershire*, Logaston Press 2005.

Porter Stephen, *Destruction in the English Civil Wars*, Sutton Publishing 1994.

Sealed Knot Souvenir Guide to The English Civil War.

Victoria County History, University of London Institute of Historical Research 1913.

Weaver Cora and Bruce Osborne, *The Illumination of St Werstan the Martyr*, Friends of Malvern Springs and Wells, 2006.

Worcestershire Village Book, Worcestershire Federation of Women's Institutes, 1988.

(And others referred to in the text)

USEFUL SOCIETIES

Discover History

Discover History is a group of Freelance Historical Interpreters covering periods from Roman/Celt – 1950s National Service. They give historical talks for societies, organise living history days for visitor attractions and history days for schools and give advice on event management. Tel: 07949222137, email: discoverhistory@aol.com, website: www. discover-history.co.uk

Parasearch

Parasearch is a regional paranormal research group founded in 1986 to investigate reports of ghosts, hauntings and poltergeists. This is a serious, scientifically-based investigative organisation for those living in Shropshire, Warwickshire, Worcestershire or the West Midlands. For further details send a stamped, self-addressed envelope to:
Parasearch
15 Brier Mill Road
Halesowen
West Midlands
B63 3HA

Photograph by Helen Lee of 'Discover History'.

Books by Anne Bradford

True Life Ghost Stories
Ghosts, Murders and Scandals I £9.95.
Ghosts, Murders and Scandals II £9.95.
Worcestershire the Haunted County £9.95.
Worcestershire Ghosts and Hauntings £9.95.
The Haunted Midlands £9.95.
Haunted Pubs of Worcestershire £7.50.
Foul Deeds and Suspicious Deaths around Worcestershire £10.99.

Oral History Books
Royal Enfield, the company and the people who made it great £14.95.
Stourport-on-Severn, a history of the town and the area £11.95.
My family and other misfits (an autobiography) £7.00.
Old Redditch being an early history of the town written by
Mr Avery between 1800 and 1850, edited by Anne Bradford £6.95.

Books by John Bradford

Severn's Southern Hills £12.95.
Shropshire's Border Hills £12.95.
The River Teme £14.95.
The River Severn £14.95.